MOBBED OUT OF EXISTENCE

MARY A. LEWIS

ISBN-13: 978-1536820225
ISBN-10: 1536820229

First Edition

CONTENTS

Workplace Colleagues in
Alphabetical Order by Last Name

Brandon Acosta — A teammate on my project team.

Steve Argon — The vice president of human resources who was in place when the bullying and mobbing occurred.

Mike Baumann — The project leader for North America.

Nicole Bennett — A teammate on my project team.

Gary Boire — The global project leader.

Adrian Bonavita — A director in the company who I knew from working in HR and who had extensive knowledge of the company and change management principles.

Stephanie Chambers — The female consultant assigned to my project team. She, along with Rick Davis, abused the power of their positions in trying to get me terminated from my job.

Rick Davis — The male vice president on the project team who, in conjunction with Stephanie Chambers, used bullying tactics to get me off the project team and out of the company.

Vicky Dennis — A teammate on my project team.

Marcus Fernandez — The CEO of the company.

Vanessa Herron — The human resources manager I spoke to about my concerns with the project.

Roberta Malvez	A human resources director who I did not know all that well but who surprisingly appeared out of nowhere to actively back up the lies of the people involved in a mobbing against me.
Kristine Marsh	A director in the company who I reported to before I was assigned to a project in which I was to lead the communications efforts. She continued to be the manager I reported to while on the project even though she herself worked outside the project.
Liz Miller	The person who was hired for my position in communications after my transfer to the project.
Ed Odom	The general counsel and chief ethics officer of the company who was my boss when I started with the company and who became part of the mobbing campaign against me.
Lynette Thames	My counterpart in communications overseas. The project was global in nature and had teams overseas that mirrored the teams in North America.
Frank Watson	The director of public relations who I knew and thought I could trust.

Worn Out Shoes

My heart has gone to what's unseen
where love is all that's real.
My eyes are sadly left behind
to see this world revealed.

I have to learn to feel my way,
and take it very slow,
in worn out shoes that barely fit
a girl from long ago.

Introduction

Everyone is familiar with bullying in the schoolyard but most of you have probably never heard of it in connection with the workplace. I certainly hadn't before experiencing it firsthand, but it is on the rise in corporate America and it is forcing honest, ethical, talented, creative and experienced people out of work with long-term personal, financial, physical and psychological difficulties that do not go away easily. In my particular experience, what began as bullying behavior by a team leader and his consultant girlfriend soon escalated to a mobbing conducted by several executives, directors, managers and the Human Resources department. Mobbing is currently defined as an accelerated form of bullying that occurs when management sides with a bullying boss and begins an orchestrated campaign to gang up on the target employee with the intent to force the employee out of the organization by libeling, isolating, harassing, terrorizing, humiliating and otherwise objectifying them.[1]

By the time I walked out of a job and career at which I excelled, my emotional and mental health was badly damaged and I was suffering from a form of Post Traumatic Stress Disorder (PTSD) called Complex PTSD. This form of PTSD is characterized by the sense of captivity felt by its sufferers. In cases of workplace mobbings, the sense of captivity is nurtured by the perpetrators of the mobbing who purposely close all doors for resolution to the targeted employee.[2]

Most of the books, articles and websites on bullying and mobbing refer to its victims as "targets." I believe the reasoning behind this is to empower them and not give them a weakened victim status. Although the employee who is abused at work is the target of someone else's bad behavior, we don't talk about victims of other traumatic events as targets of rape, targets of murder, targets of domestic abuse, etc. In writing this book, I refer to myself as a target when I write from the viewpoint of the people who bullied and ganged up on me but I never lose sight of the fact that I was an assault victim in every sense of the word and it wasn't until I was able to reestablish my own sense of worth and gain back some of the confidence and emotional stability they stole from me that I no longer felt like a victim. Complete recovery of your emotional well being is difficult, however. Victims of mobbing always suffer some kind of psychological damage and the effects of PTSD can linger for a lifetime.

When I was finally able to talk about the experience many months afterward, one person I spoke to thought I was having hard time getting over people being mean to me. I have a suspicion this is a view held by many people because there is so little awareness about bullying and mobbing in the workplace. This perception frustrates me to no end because there is a distinct difference between people who are mean and adults who are willing to psychologically assault someone to further their own selfish agendas. And make no mistake about it. Bullying and mobbing behaviors are forms of psychological assault. Workplace bullying is not about people who are ambitious, tough or hard driving. It is about narcissistic and weak people who will objectify and abuse an employee in an effort to weaken them so that they themselves look better in comparison.

In my case, the assault began when I accepted a new assignment and started working on a global project with Rick Davis, a vice president who was brought in from a different location to lead our team. When Rick's actions escalated into a gang style mobbing for reasons I will get into when I tell my story; his allies in management, some of my co-workers and the HR department all aligned themselves with him in an effort to run me out of the company. The use of the word "mobbing" may seem strange but that is exactly what it was. They lost all sense of reason as individuals and let the group think that characterizes a mob mentality take over. Once their campaign against me was set in motion, my chances of survival with my well being intact were slim to none. I was completely blind-sided and a good portion of this book is dedicated to helping anyone facing a similar situation to be aware of what is happening to them while it is happening so that every action they take is taken to protect themselves – body, mind and soul. In the case of bullying and mobbing, hindsight is not 20/20. It is crucial to be aware of the types of thought patterns and behavior that characterize what we call bullying and mobbing so that you can prepare your mind beforehand for the assault that is about to take place against it. Preparation is the only cure for the devastating effects these behaviors have on the human mind.

One of the difficulties bullying and mobbing victims have is talking about the experience. This may be why so little is heard about this phenomenon. I have no doubt that the perpetrators use this to their advantage. This book was a very long time in the making. It was extremely difficult to write because I hate thinking about these people and what they did to me. It would have been so much easier to bury the entire experience in the recesses of my mind somewhere and pretend like it never happened. I believe I may have done just that if I had been able to find a job and focus on something else in the aftermath, but unfortunately the perpetrators' own actions made it impossible for me to do that.

So by now, you might be asking yourself what I did to deserve such treatment. Like most rational people, you would naturally conclude that there must have been some reason for them to gang up on me since adults don't bully other adults, particularly when they are responsible members of management in a corporate environment. You would be right in the sense that in most civilized environments people will treat their fellow human beings with some degree of civility and respect. It is how we are all able to get along with one another on a day-to-day basis. However, the environment I was in was neither civilized nor rational, but the individuals who mobbed me hid behind a very rational and civil set of company values. If an employee was not aware of the alternate reality these people really operated in, they set themselves for all sorts of misery. When the chief ethics officer and general counsel is a member of the mob, then you know you have real problems.

The fact of the matter is that I did not do anything wrong. I was a stellar employee working for a company I loved and to which I felt very loyal. My job was everything to me. When my love for the company and my own passion for my job and career became the catalysts for speaking up about what I believed to be the mismanagement of the project, I unknowingly released a volcano that had been quietly brewing beneath the surface of a company that was preaching one message and practicing a very different one. The molten lava of corruption that had heretofore been contained with the strategies of bullying and mobbing I describe in this book to keep all dissenters and truth tellers silenced was released upon me with a vengeance because the truth I told touched upon each and every corrupt bone in the managerial body of this hypocritical company.

There are no easy answers to solving the problem of bullying in either our workplaces or schools. Every book, article, website, blog and forum on bullying provide different ideas for tackling it and none of those ideas are surefire solutions to preventing or eliminating it. No one came to my rescue and in most cases of bullying you can pretty much assume that's a given. Until the culture of the American workplace changes and decides it will be in its best (and most profitable) interest to replace false and dangerous management practices with rational ones that respect the dignity of all people, then you are on your own out there. It is incumbent upon you to face the reality of the situation as quickly as possible and do whatever you need to do to keep your confidence and mental health intact when the odds are so steeply stacked against you.

If this book accomplishes nothing else, I want people reading it to begin noticing patterns of thought and behavior used by all the people, including myself, in this story of workplace abuse. I want them to begin putting the puzzle pieces together because putting the puzzle pieces of human thought and behavior together is what eventually saved my mind, soul and body – all of which were in need of intensive healing after the mental and emotional beating they took from people out to protect their own self interests at all costs.

I now realize that I am just one of millions and billions of people who have suffered similar assaults to their psyches over the course of history at the hands of people abusing their personal power to assault them at will. My love goes out to all the men and women who have found themselves within the target range of a power abuser. My prayer is that if you should ever find yourself caught up in this battle in which there are never any winners, you survive and thrive with the knowledge that you have everything you need for combat. The person who is assaulting your sense of well being chose you because you are better than him in every possible way. Keep that knowledge in your soul and never let go of it. It will lead you to ultimate victory.

Laws Fail When A Gang Holds The Power

The Bullying Begins When I Start A New Assignment

I was a 54-year old professional woman working in job at which I excelled and in a career I loved when I discovered I have no power whatsoever when corrupt people are in charge. I had been working as a communications specialist for just over four years when I was asked to lead the communications efforts for a global software project. I worked very hard at becoming good at what I did, even spending much of my free time outside of work learning all I could about marketing and communications. For the first time ever in my professional career, most of which was spent in the legal field, I found myself in a job where I was able to explore my own creativity through my work. I was a strong writer and had always been good at using words to communicate a message, but increasingly I was discovering how what we see visually can have just as much impact on us as the written word. I began to teach myself graphic design in order to study how images and color could be used more effectively in delivering messages to employees. By the time I was asked to lead the communications efforts in North America for this project, I was already designing many of the layouts for the company's magazine and communications campaigns.

Everything I was learning and discovering about visual communication was making me think about how those same techniques could be used in the classroom environment. I decided that I wanted to pursue a master's degree in education, with a specialization in instructional design, in order to pursue a teaching career upon my retirement. I already had a bachelor's degree in English and I had earned an associate's degree in computer programming a few years earlier; all of which gave me a good, solid foundation for learning computer-based design. I was also planning on using my experience on the project to transition to a role in training and development once the project was over. A degree in education and instructional design would fit nicely in my new career path and would aid me in finding more inventive and innovative ways to present information in my current role.

I wholeheartedly bought into the American dream that told me if I planned right and worked hard, I could achieve anything I set my sight upon. I came very close to achieving my American dream when I came face-to-face with real evil in the form of a group of work colleagues I considered to be good people. For this gang, the American dream was theirs to grant or deny. They decided who succeeded and who was disposable. Success in this company had nothing to do with talent, dedication, hard work, knowledge or experience and everything to do with who the group in charge liked, who was willing to play their deceitful games and who was willing to sell their integrity for the price of a job. In this environment, dreams were achieved at the price of your soul – a price I was unwilling to pay.

What we have labeled as bullying doesn't only destroy a person's ego, confidence, self esteem, mental acuity and overall sense of well being; it also kills their dreams. All my plans and goals were stopped dead in their tracks once Rick decided to target me. I didn't know much about Rick before joining the project. He had come from another location within the company and I had only met him once before, during a brief visit there for a meeting I was attending. He struck me as very personable as he chatted it up with our group and showed us around. My impression of him didn't change much in the early days of the project. He was always very pleasant in our meetings and I even recall telling my supervisor that I liked him when she asked me how it was working with him. It took me several weeks before realizing that his exterior display of pleasantries and his propensity for talking were merely ploys he used to cover up his inability to engage and lead a team focused on change management. I have a feeling he spent many years perfecting his easy going manner so he could use it to fool people and keep them from getting to know the real man beneath the facade.

Rick could talk and talk and talk as he so often did in our team meetings. Initially, I thought he knew what he was talking about, but it soon became apparent that he was merely parroting what was being told to him by the consultant assigned to our team. He once commented to us that he had become known for his long meetings at his previous location where he was no doubt parroting what was said in all the leadership meetings the company had for its officers. I suppose that trick worked well enough for him there where things probably ran themselves to a great extent. Now he was in a completely new role where he had to come up with the processes on his own. He was at a complete loss as to where to even start. The job required good communication skills, a long-range view and a willingness on Rick's part to elicit and incorporate ideas from the team. Rick wasn't a long-range thinker and although a great talker, he wasn't much of a communicator. His background was in accounting and he was a controller before becoming a vice president on the operations side of the business. He was not trained in change management and expressed to me on a couple of occasions how hard it was for him to deal with the people side of change and the inevitable personal issues that arise from it. This difficulty manifested itself very strongly in how he approached his new role. He simply didn't know how to effectively lead a team and fell back on his "I'm in charge here" persona whenever he felt threatened about his insecurities getting exposed.

A balanced person – when faced with a situation in which he finds himself lacking in the requisite skills – will recognize that deficit and either acquire the knowledge he needs to perform the work required of him, or will rely on others with the requisite skills to help him achieve his objectives. Bullies are anything but balanced. Too lazy to put forth the effort required for attaining the skills they need to be competent in their work, bullies prefer to take the easy way out and mask their inadequacies with superficial qualities that are looked upon favorably by people who can help them move up the corporate hierarchy. Workplace bullies are masters at playing the game of office politics - the web like underbelly of many American corporations. Knowing that the spoils go to those who play the game the best, bullies become adept at using office politics to help them get to where they want to go. They have learned how to weave and flatter their way to positions for which they are wholly unqualified, but which move them further up the corporate hierarchy.

I have no doubt that office politics and the likability factor played a huge role in Rick's ascent within the corporation, which was unfortunate for him because eventually he found himself in a place where his gift for gab no longer worked so well in masking his inadequacies. Luckily for him, Rick had Stephanie Chambers who was more than willing to come to his rescue. Stephanie was the consultant assigned to our particular team. As the project was global in nature, there were various teams assembled over two continents focused on different areas of the software implementation. Our team's job was to get employees adjusted to all the changes the new system would bring to their work areas. We not only needed to make them aware that their old systems were being replaced; we also needed to get them talking positively about the new system and make them excited about all the changes it would bring to them personally and to the company as a whole.

Both Rick and Stephanie had a strong desire to hold onto what they knew and were familiar with. They were basically two people put in charge of managing change who themselves were unwilling and/or unable to change and adapt their work styles to suit the environment in which they found themselves. Stephanie in particular took a one-size fits all approach and had trouble adjusting to the culture of the company. She insisted on using all the same materials and following the same approach her company used for all their jobs. Rick just followed her cue because through mimicking what she told him, he could appear to know what he was talking about. This actually suited him quite well because he was nothing of a thinker. He was a repeater and doer. There was never any discussion about anything at all. Rick and Stephanie made all the decisions themselves without any input from the other team members. We were a team in name only.

Like many other uncreative minds found in the corporate environment, Rick and Stephanie channeled their efforts into learning how to play the game of office politics. Stephanie knew the political game inside out and played it like a black belt. Although not as cunning and sharp as Stephanie, Rick knew the subtleties of how the game was played in this particular office environment. He also knew the people who could be potential allies for the two of them.

Even though their personal objectives mirrored one another, Stephanie and Rick were two different personality types entirely. Rick was clearly not up to the job and compensated for it by talking a lot so as to appear like he was in charge. Stephanie was far more complex. She actually did know her stuff and was very capable. I admired that about her. It wasn't until much later that I realized it allowed her to hide behind her mask much more effectively. Her mask was black and impenetrable. It lured me in. I couldn't help but like her. Along with being very smart and well spoken, she was very pleasant to be around. She always came to work smiling and with a funny story to tell. Her easy going manner and approachability made it very easy for me to confide in her when problems began to surface with Rick. That gave them an incredible advantage in the war they waged against me in secret.

I cannot say what the personal dynamic was between the two of them was but I can say that Rick's inabilities in dealing with conflict, a major part of his job as team lead for change management, made him very dependent on Stephanie. It was a match literally made in hell. I can't help but think how different my life would be now if fate had not brought Rick and Stephanie together. They fed off each other like parasites, each providing the other with the qualities they needed to feed their desires for control and glory. They were able to hide behind the other one's strong points. If Rick had been forced to figure things out on his own, it would have quickly become apparent he was inadequate for the job. If Stephanie had been paired up with a strong leader who knew what he was doing, she would have been relegated to the position she was hired for in the first place – that of a consultant and not the harassing boss title that Rick allowed her to assume.

Unlike Rick, Stephanie was not an employee of the company but due to Rick's lack of knowledge about change and project management, she quickly assumed a kind of unwritten managerial position. Stephanie had a vast knowledge of the software and its application – knowledge that none of the rest of us had. Much of the material she provided contained terms we were completely unfamiliar with and she was the go-to person for understanding it. Stephanie thrived on being the one everyone went to with questions. She loved doling out the information because it gave her control over how much she would share with anyone at any given time. Stephanie was all about control: control of information, control of work, control of planning and control of people. She controlled it all. She was very confident and domineering and took a very aggressive approach to controlling all aspects of the team's work.

However, it is not possible to control someone who isn't willing to be controlled and Rick was more than happy to fit the bill. He would never allow himself to admit this of course and his denial was what made him so dangerous. For Rick, acting like he was in charge was sufficient. His failure to deal with his own insecurities made it impossible to improve the working environment while he was there. Rick wasn't interested in improving anything if it risked leaving him exposed. He lived in a world where appearances were all that counted and as long as he had Stephanie for cover, nothing else mattered. The dynamic between the two of them always made me wonder how Stephanie worked with her company's other clients. What would she have done if she had been paired up with a team leader who knew as much as her about change management? She didn't have to worry about that with Rick though. He relied on her to do the job of making them both look good, no matter the price anyone else had to pay. It wasn't long before we all determined that Stephanie was going to be the one calling all the shots on how the implementation would progress and we fell in line just like the automatons they wanted us to be. The consultant became the boss over the employees of a company that hired her for consulting services. That was just the beginning of the screwy world Rick created with the help of his executive buddies to hide his incompetence.

During the time I worked with Stephanie and Rick, I kept trying to figure why they treated me the way they did. It became an obsession. But no more. Those days are over. It doesn't matter what their motivations were. They were a couple of workplace bullies, pure and simple. Their motives could be any number of things, but the end result was the same. My career ended and my personal health and well being began to steadily decline as soon as they targeted me and my job.

I should have known better but I took people at face value. I viewed the workplace like any other place and failed to account for the fact that it is a competitive environment filled with competitive people wanting to advance and succeed in their careers. Some people take a fair and honest approach and others are more manipulative and willing to work the system. They have no problem with using people in a manner that serves their own self interests rather than the mission of the company or any common goals. Unless a company is dedicated to upholding its mission and values and works diligently to ensure that all its managers and employees are on the same page with regard to its mission and values, then a corrupt leader who has climbed the ladder through means other than ability, intelligence and skills can very easily lead it down an alternate path and managers can very easily fall in line behind him/her. It is simply a reality of the modern-day workplace and all employees should be aware of this reality going in.

Although Rick was not a leader in any sense of the word, he had a title and that was enough to intimidate Kristine Marsh, my manager in Communications who I continued reporting to while assigned to the project team. Even though she herself was a director of the corporation, she always took a very subservient stance in her interactions with the vice presidents and CEO of the company, all of whom loved Rick and gave him their tacit endorsement when he began telling lies about me. Kristine was my manager and she was well aware of Rick's malicious lies about me but she was not about to confront him or any of the other executives who supported him, even if it required her to lie and harm me in the worst possible ways. In that sense, she became the biggest bully of them all and the most dangerous as it turns out to my safety and well being. She should have protected me when I continually went to her with my concerns. Instead, she abandoned me and sided with the group of executives who lied, schemed, plotted and destroyed my professional career and personal reputation to save their own corrupt and cowardly ones.

I use the word 'bullying' to describe their behavior, but when they were employing their tactics against me I didn't have a name for what was happening to me. I am still not certain that bullying is the right term to use, although it has become the accepted terminology in most of the literature on this form of gender neutral harassment in the workplace. The underlying goal of bullying is the same in all its forms and that is to hide one's own inadequacies and insecurities by humiliating and dehumanizing the target of the abuse. The results can be equally devastating whether it occurs in the school yard or workplace. Although bullying by teachers against students does occur (I describe such a case that happened with my son later on in the book) most of the bullying taking place in schools is between fellow students where the power of the individuals is evenly distributed from a structural point of view. In the workplace, where most bullying is done by a supervisor against a subordinate, the power is unevenly distributed.[3] Given these power dynamics, many of the practices used for combating bullying in our schools are ineffective in a working environment.

However, I should qualify that assertion by pointing out that many of the strategies for combating bullying in the school setting are also proving to be ineffective and are in fact providing bullies with new and inventive ways to harass their victims in ways they hadn't thought of before. The reason why rehabilitation and therapy do not work on criminal psychopathic types is because they do not believe they did anything wrong. Their minds have already turned their victims into people who deserved it. Bullying and mobbing is, by its very nature, psychopathic behavior. If a bully views his target as the bad guy who deserves the treatment he are dishing out but the bully has people telling him that he is the problem, the natural reaction is to be defensive. Human nature is to self protect so that the image we have of ourselves is protected. To have a teacher, principal or parent call us out as a bully results in personal denial and feelings of wanting to retaliate against the person who tarnished our image in the eyes of others. Telling a victim of bullying to report it could be the worst possible advice to give because it causes the bully to become vengeful. In order to prevent further damage to his public image, the bully personality will go underground and begin manipulating and abusing the target in the dark where there are no witnesses. In my case, I told my manager, the HR manager, the attorney and ethics officer of the company and my colleague about Rick's abusive behavior and nothing was done. As I describe later, Rick went underground and got me in a room alone with him where it would be his word against mine when he would try to level a charge of insubordination against me.

I have come to believe that the label we have given to this behavior was a terrible mistake. Bullying behavior is human behavior acted out by disordered minds. Putting these people under the bully umbrella creates a whole new layer of problems. A few months after leaving my job and discovering there was a name for what Rick and Stephanie did to me, I tried taking a survey about bullying. The survey gave many different scenarios and asked whether the responder would consider them acts of bullying. I had to stop taking the survey halfway through because the situations they provided were listed one by one, with each example providing a clear behavior. For example, if your boss yells at you, is that bullying; or if you are excluded from meetings, is that bullying? Well, it may be and it may not be. It is very hard to define because it is not just one or two incidents or variables that constitute bullying behavior. You have to analyze the types of activities being complained of, the number of occurrences, the personalities of the people involved, both parties' version of events, the length of time it has been going on, when it started, why it started and a host of other factors. Even if a company does a thorough investigation, which most do not, things can be missed. Bullies are adept at determining what their victims' vulnerabilities are and attacking them through subterfuge. They are too cowardly to ever come right out and say up front how they feel about their targets and they are incapable of looking inward at themselves to determine why they feel the way they do about them. Instead, they hide their aggression in words that sound reasonable to an outsider, but are deliberately chosen to let the victim know where her place is.

In their book, *Bully at Work*, Gary and Ruth Namie (a victim of workplace bullying herself) describe in vivid detail how in a matter of months, a talented, healthy, competent and confident employee can be driven out of a job and to financial, physical and emotional ruin at the hands of a bully who is supported by an employer. That was certainly true in my case. I began working with Rick in mid-April and walked out (before they had the opportunity to terminate me) in mid-September. I wouldn't have thought it possible, but in five short months I went from being a confident, talented, motivated and creative writer and communications specialist pursuing a master's degree in education; to being unemployed, separated from my husband, unable to continue in the master's program and dropping out, completely broken emotionally and questioning whether I wanted to live anymore. It sounds like a nightmare scenario, but this is a common outcome for many victims of workplace bullying and/or mobbing. Assessing the situation as a personality conflict between two people, as human resources departments most always do, is dead wrong. Personality conflicts occur between two colleagues possessing the same level of power. In the majority of workplace bullying cases, the bully is a superior who holds power over the subordinate target. When the bullying continues unabated due to the unwillingness of human resources and/or management to intervene, victims soon find themselves without support as colleagues abandon them out of fear of becoming victims themselves. Family and friends also may not be able to provide much needed help because they really don't understand what bullying and mobbing is or what it does to a person's mind. Many times, they grow tired of listening to stories about what the bully is doing and will often encourage their family member to compromise and try to get along with the bully as best they can. That is the advice I received from my own father, who had my best interests at heart but couldn't possibly understand how I was being treated. He had been the director of public relations for a non-profit before he retired and he still remained in contact with people who had worked for him 34 years earlier. After he died, one of his employees sent me an email telling me what a great boss my father was and how he had mentored her right out of college and throughout her career at the company. The idea that someone would purposely set out to to take someone's job away from them, destroy their confidence and then kill their chances of finding another job by giving a bad reference was as foreign to my father as it was to me.

That is exactly what workplace power abusers do and they not only do not feel bad about it, they receive a perverse kind of thrill in watching their target's emotional, mental and professional decline. They are disordered personalities who, despite outward appearances, have low self-esteem and are insecure in their own abilities but are too lazy to do anything about it. Many of them have climbed the corporate ladder for reasons other than competence and ability to do their jobs. When they find themselves in positions for which they are unqualified, they rely on old habits and refuse to take responsibility for acquiring the skills they need to properly fulfill their new job roles. They have no problem, however, with accepting the salary bump that goes along with each progressive position.

Targets of these harassers are almost always more capable, competent and willing to do and learn whatever it takes to get the job done well for the employer without compromising their own sense of integrity or personal set of values. These qualities make them very confident individuals and bullies hate them for it. They seethe with envy because the target is everything they are not. Out of fear that some of the glory they so desperately crave may go to the target, they begin a campaign to break down the target's confidence in herself and demean her abilities in the eyes of colleagues. Since the power is usually in their hands, bullies have an arsenal of tactics they can use in their shell game of hiding their own inadequacies to make it appear like it is the more competent and less powerful target who is inadequate. Bullies will knit pick, fault find, micromanage, constantly correct, overwork, under-work, misinform, set unreasonable deadlines, isolate, ignore, give bad performance evaluations, withhold resources and do or say anything else they need to in order to wear down their targets and make them begin to doubt themselves and their abilities.

Bullying in the workplace is never about just one or two incidents. It is repetitive, malicious behavior aimed at destroying an employee's sense of purpose and well being. In my case, the initial attacks on my work were very subtle in nature. A few months into the campaign, when the bullying transitioned into a mobbing conducted by human resources, members of management and a couple of upper level executives, it became an all-out frontal attack to take my job away from me and get me out of the company.

Patterns of thought and behavior we have labeled as bullying and mobbing are simply corrupted patterns of thought and behavior. That is why it will be impossible to ever legislate the problem away. It is overall bad behavior used by corrupt people operating in corrupt systems to benefit their own self interests. Like murderers, rapists, thieves and extortionists; we have tried to classify these kinds of people in the workplace by giving them the name "bullies" so they can be separated out and dealt with. However, in the corporate system I was in, the people occupying the top rows of the hierarchy were able to paint me as the bullying trouble maker and I was the only one who was punished. We risk turning the tables on good people if we try to legislate this problem away. That is exactly what was done in Nazi Germany with the Final Solution to deal with the "trouble making Jews." Although everyone can agree that Hitler was an evil man, Hitler himself believed he was doing the work of God.[3] To the victors go not only the spoils, but also the ability to control the narrative. History is written and rewritten by people at the top of society's hierarchies and people like me have to deal with the false legacies they create for us.

Bullying and mobbing are insidious behaviors for which there are simply no easy answers because the root cause for the behavior is human nature. Rules, regulations and laws may prevent it or stop it from happening in some instances, but they will never eradicate the problem completely because it is a human problem. I was a 54-year old woman protected by age discrimination and anti-harassment laws and it still happened to me. As with any difficult problem, finding a solution for ending bullying in all its forms will require an understanding of why it happens in the first place by identifying the patterns of thought that cause people to engage in the behavior and by creating an awareness in people's minds of the devastating effects the behavior has on the intended targets of it.

My experience is probably an exception rather than the rule as few bullying cases become full fledged mobbings where the resources of the organization are garnered against the target. In many cases, the bullying can go on for years before the target decides she can't take it anymore and either transfers to another department, quits or is terminated. Bullied targets have a 70 percent chance that they will lose their jobs, either voluntarily or through constructive discharge, after being targeted. In only 13 percent of cases are perpetrators punished or terminated.[4] However, in all cases of workplace bullying, it is probably safe to say that the bullying begins when an insecure person (usually a supervisor or manager) decides it will serve his self-interests to downgrade the qualities, talents and experience of someone under him because they make him look bad in comparison.

That is certainly how my story began and how countless others have and will begin.

2

Tactics Used By Bullies Are Universal

Bullying Is A Series of Incidents Used To Trivialize Target's Abilities

I have become an expert on workplace bullying the hard way. I didn't know anything about it when my supervisor, Kristine Marsh, unexpectedly called me into a meeting to tell me I was chosen to lead employee communications for a global two-year project the company was undertaking. The news came as a complete surprise to me and I think I was in a state of disbelief for a couple of days. The communications department had been preparing articles, speeches and other materials for the previous year or so touting the importance of this project for the company. It was going to touch every aspect of the business and they made no secret about the importance of choosing the right people to ensure its success. I definitely viewed it as an honor to be chosen as one of the members of the team. After providing a brief explanation of what my role would entail, Kristine told me to think about it for a couple of days and let her know what I wanted to do. I didn't need a couple of days. I knew as soon as I walked out the door that I would accept it. I got more and more excited as I thought about the opportunities that could open up for me by working on a project of this magnitude.

I started working at the company four years earlier as a legal administrator working for Ed Odom, the company's general counsel and chief ethics officer. I worked for him for several months before transferring to a different department and position. He later played a major role in the mobbing against me. Other than Kristine, I blame him the most for the devastating consequences the experience had on my family and life. It was his job to investigate and resolve just these kinds of circumstances. Instead he ignored everything I told him when I reached out to him in a desperate plea for help and then turned the tables on me in the most reprehensible way. His complete disregard for me and what I told him could have had devastating consequences for the company if I had been a different kind of person. Bullying and mobbing are behind many workplace shootings, as evidenced by the rash of postal shootings that all traced back to bully managers. It is also my belief it could have had a devastating impact on the company's profitability; not only in terms of a bad project installation that would have resulted in continual costs down the road but also in terms of a lawsuit that had the potential for a significant payout since I was in a couple of protected classes and had the sense to document and save all the emails that traced the harassment and negligence from start to finish. As it turns out, they were more than willing to sacrifice me but heed the advice I gave them regarding the mismanagement of the project. People don't get any more selfish and self interested than the managers in this company, but I'll get into all that later.

In my eyes, leading the communications efforts in North America for a global project was a huge milestone given where I had started. That is not to say I didn't have a healthy dose of trepidation about accepting the assignment. It was going to be a big step. Although I would be working with a team of people, I knew that I would be the main person responsible for making key recommendations with regard to communications for the project. At that point, I was not aware that I would have a counterpart outside of North America who would be working closely with me. I thought it would all fall in my hands and I was a little nervous that I might not be up to the task.

A short time after talking to Kristine about the assignment, I took the elevator down to the lobby with Roberta Malvez. Roberta was an HR director who had done a lot of work in choosing people for the project teams. I knew everyone in human resources because the internal communications responsibilities for the company were contained within the HR department. Roberta congratulated me and we chatted for a few minutes on our way out of the building. I told her how excited I was about having been chosen, but also that I was a little nervous and didn't really understand how they would utilize someone full-time for communications. Communications responsibilities for all the other company initiatives were always handled by the employees themselves, in coordination with Marketing and Communications. Having worked on job roles for the project, Roberta was very familiar with what would be required of me and was actually quite helpful with the information she provided. This was the last of less than a handful of times I ever spoke to Roberta. I mention this because her name pops up later in a very unexpected way.

After telling Kristine I was on board, I met with Rick and Mike Baumann. Mike was the project manager in North America. I think they were both a little taken aback at my enthusiasm and that may have been part of my undoing. I may have put too much value on this transfer. If asked at the time why I was so excited about it, I think I would have attributed it to the strong desire I had to advance in my career and the perception I had that this was a step in that direction. I think Rick must have had a similar expectation or he never would have given up his prestigious role as the vice president in charge of a location.

In the months that followed my initial meeting with Rick and Mike, Rick would periodically ask me if I was still as enthusiastic about everything as I was when I first met with the two of them. I assumed he just wanted to make sure I was happy and content. He seemed like that kind of guy. There was no way I could have guessed that his inquiries were a way of gauging how successful he and Stephanie were in their campaign against me. From outward appearances, Rick was very unassuming. He looked like the nerd you sat next to in high school, not the bully in the back row. He was Mr. All-Around-Nice-Guy and it made it hard for me to accept him for who he really was. I kept questioning myself and thinking he couldn't possibly be as inept as I thought he was. He wasn't. Rick was a passive-aggressive personality type and I miscalculated him at every turn. I was thinking I could interact with him like I did my colleagues in communications and express my opinions openly. However, open communication with a passive aggressive person is like oil to water. You will never pierce the smiling face they present to the world because it is their shield. Their smile is a two-edged sword. Beneath the surface is a person who is seething with hidden resentments and insecurities which they are unable, or unwilling, to express verbally. If you happen to be in their cross hairs for something you have done or someone you are (in the case of a target, someone who is more competent and talented) they will cut you in two through sabotage and not leave a trace. The one skill they have put effort into perfecting is their ability to lie and avoid responsibility.

Part of their MO is the thrill they get from seeing you driven to distraction trying to figure them out. I gave Rick just what he was looking for right up until the end and by then it was too late to change course or strategy in dealing with him. I think it was his behind-the-scenes campaign to demean my abilities and work ethic that helped him succeed in acquiring a gang of managers, executives and bystanders ready and willing to join with him in forcing me out of the company and career I loved. There is a passage in the Bible that reads, "There are three things I dread and a fourth which terrifies me: Public slander, the gathering of a mob, and false accusation – all harder to bear than death."[5] One insecure little man with no honor, integrity, honesty or sense of fair play was able to wreak havoc all around him with his lies. Not one of those managers or executives or bystanders ever bothered to have a single conversation with me about what Rick was saying, nor did they offer me any support or solace as they saw me slowly coming apart at the seams.

Rick and Stephanie had their strategy for undermining me mapped out almost from day one. In the beginning, their efforts were directed at making me lose confidence in myself and making others believe I was incompetent in my role. As they stepped up their campaign of personal and professional destruction several months later, it was in a desperate attempt to keep their own professional negligence from coming to light.

I remember clearly an incident that happened early on in the project which was insignificant at the time, but was definitely a sign of things to come. Rick and I were talking in my cubicle when a director in the organization came by and joined the conversation. I had worked with him before on various projects when I was in human resources and we got along very well. The three of us began chatting and at one point in the conversation, the director looked at Rick and said (referring to me), "She is the best in her field." Now, my natural response to such a comment would be to say something like, "I know. We are very happy to have her on the team," or words to that effect. Rick didn't respond that way at all. He didn't say anything at all in reply. He just continued on with something else and walked away shortly thereafter. His response, or I should say non-response, was really no big deal and I dismissed it at the time without giving it much thought. It was one of those totally minor things that people do everyday that you just throw off and don't think about twice. I only remember this conversation because it made me feel really good when the director said it and I mention it now because it was the first incident in a series of incidents that had the cumulative effect of trivializing my abilities and undermining my confidence.

Rick's tactics were very subtle and hard to identify even as they were being employed against me. As a matter of fact, I attributed most of them to what I perceived as Rick's inadequacy for the job and I felt bad for him. It is very hard to forge a counterattack when you are not aware you are being attacked in the first place. All I had to go on was a vague sense that things were not right. I couldn't figure out if maybe I was making more of it than I should, or if it was the way things should be and I shouldn't be making anything of it at all. When I would try to talk to Rick about it, he would act like he understood my concerns but then I'd leave the room realizing nothing had changed.

The project was well underway when I joined the team. All the other team members had already attended a week long orientation that covered project scope and time line for delivery. Soon after I came on board, Stephanie sent me some of the presentations they went over during the orientation. After reviewing them, I arranged to meet with her to talk about them. I wanted her to explain how she had helped other companies implement similar projects in the past so that I could have a better understanding of the kinds of communications that would be required.

Stephanie showed her true colors in this first meeting, but I failed to recognize the signs. When I started the meeting off by asking her for an overview of the project, she responded by pleasantly asking me, "Didn't you review the presentations I sent you?" I had reviewed them, but they were very technical in nature and focused more on the software itself than on the project phases or implementation. I automatically felt like I must have missed something and in an effort not to appear stupid, I began asking her questions about some of the unfamiliar technical terms I had jotted down during my review. She happily explained them to me and then commended me for "asking such good questions." No overview was offered and no plan for going forward was ever discussed. I left the meeting with an uneasy feeling that I had missed something, so I went back to my desk to review the presentations several times again. I confirmed that there was nothing in them about how similar projects were implemented at other companies, nor did they provide any specific information about communications and messaging that would have been valuable for me to know in terms of anticipating future activities. This was a pattern of evasion, misdirection and table turning that would be followed throughout my time on the project, by both her, Rick and ultimately the other members of the mob.

For someone reading the previous paragraph, their natural inclination might be to question why I didn't just stay there until she gave me the overview I requested in the first place. Other than the fact that I don't believe she ever would have offered it and instead would have followed her pattern of saying she had a meeting to attend or a phone call to take when she was being pushed for information, the reason why I didn't do that is hard to explain. It is why bullying behavior is so insidious. Bullies have a clear goal in mind. They are usually insecure individuals who do not want anyone stealing the spotlight from them. In Stephanie's case, insecurities didn't drive her, but power through control of information did. Stephanie went into that meeting knowing exactly the kind of information I wanted from her and she knew it wasn't contained in the slides I reviewed. I went into that meeting thinking she was the expert who had done these implementations multiple times before and would not hesitate sharing what she knew with me so that I could be effective in my job. When I asked her for an overview and she (the expert) responded by directing me to the slides, I automatically assumed I must have missed something. We all have pride to a greater or lesser degree. Since this was one of my first encounters with Stephanie and she didn't know me or my background, I didn't want her to think she was working with an idiot.

In order to look like I had some level of intelligence, I improvised by asking her about some of the terms I had written down. Even now I question myself because it is hard to believe that people can be this calculating – but they are.

Dismissive Of Work Product

One of the main goals the company hoped to achieve with the initiative was uniformity in its global business operations. The project was structured so that the teams responsible for determining how work processes were performed in the North American locations mirrored the teams that were put together at other locations and given the same task. Together, all these teams would come up with a single set of best practices to create a unified world class business system. Lynette Thames was my mirror counterpart in communications overseas. I was first introduced to Lynette during a telephone conference call Rick, Stephanie and I had with her and the other members of her team. It was right after I started and I was still not totally clear on what would be required of me. All I remember about the call is that Lynette sounded absolutely ecstatic over having me on the project. She was anxious for me to look over a communications plan she had created for the first phase of the project which would take place outside of North America. The plan she put together was perfect and didn't need any input from me but she sent it to me anyway. Lynette always included me in whenever she was working on materials regarding global project communications. Even when she didn't take my advice, she always made me feel like my opinion was valuable.

Soon after the phone conversation with Lynette and her team, I traveled overseas to work on the communications plan that would serve as the foundation for our communications efforts throughout the entire project. Shortly after I arrived in town, Lynette wanted to meet with me just so we could get to know one another. During the course of our conversation, Lynette asked me how I liked working with Kristine. I just gave an automatic response like she was good to work for and Lynette said something like, "Oh, nobody down here likes her." I never bothered to ask her why they didn't like her. I do this all the time and every time I do, I want to hit rewind. Instead of following up on statements that require follow-up, I just let them hang out there and then later wonder why the person said what they did. I can't really say why I do this except to say it is one of my faults I am working very hard on correcting. It really worked against me in viewing the situation and the people involved realistically rather than the way I wanted them to be or thought they should be because of their position titles and job roles. It prevented me from standing my ground with Stephanie in our initial meeting and it kept me blind to the weak and cowardly character of my manager. Lynette was anything but a bully, but I wanted to point out this habit of mine not to question and follow up because it worked in Rick and Stephanie's favor. I never made them explain themselves.

For any other targets who suffer from this habit, for whatever reason, change it immediately. Start asking lots of questions. If you don't get a satisfactory answer to your question, ask another question or ask it differently. People who abuse the power of their positions love to keep instructions and assignments unclear so that it looks like you don't understand the subject matter. Hold the bully's feet to the fire at all times so that both of you have clarity. By doing this, it will help prevent the person abusing the power of his position from turning the tables on you and making it look like you don't know what you're doing. Force confrontation when you realize a supervisor is using tactics like Stephanie used. If they say they have a phone call to take or a meeting to attend when you are asking for critical information you need to do your job properly, then follow up with them. Arrange a time that is good for them when they have no phone calls to take or meetings to attend. Have your questions ready for them and do not leave the meeting room without answers. This is the time to remain confident in yourself and your abilities because they will try manipulating and intimidating you into submitting to the less competent peon label they have mentally given you. They have perfected the art of condescension with their looks of disbelief in your ignorance and words that sound good on the surface but are meant to undercut your confidence in the skills you have worked so hard at attaining.

Stephanie was extremely good with the looks of disbelief while Rick always liked using hidden digs to keep me in my place. At one point, Mike asked me to write a letter for him. After drafting it, I sent a copy to Rick and Mike for review. Although Mike was fine with it, Rick suggested I send it to Kristine to look over. Other than the fact that English was not Kristine's first language and she relied on me to do all the writing while I worked with her in Communications, she was not involved in the project and there was no reason for her to review any of my work for the project. The only reason he suggested it was to minimize my abilities.

The trip overseas ended with Lynette and I accomplishing what we set out to do and I went home with a communications plan that could be used for the entire length of the project. Upon my return to the states, I scheduled some time with Rick and Stephanie to go over the plan that Lynette and I put together. I wanted to get their input and fill in any gaps we may have missed. Lynette and I had organized the plan by project phases, each of which was expected to last for several months. After presenting the plan to Stephanie and Rick, Stephanie suggested breaking out the items listed under each phase and putting dates by them to indicate when each would get done. All I had been given up to this point was a bar chart showing the project phases. We never talked about dates in our overview meeting and Stephanie never provided any specific information with regard to the timing of the project phases or the activities involved with each.

Since she wasn't furthering the discussion by offering any ideas of her own as to when she anticipated these communications occurring, I agreed to take a look at it and the meeting was adjourned. Rick didn't offer any feedback at all.

This was to be the plan for communications throughout the entire project and nothing was discussed about it except for Stephanie's suggestion of dates, and a few formatting changes on the Power Point. I had expected us to go through it item by item; refining messages, timing of communications, the best type of communication material for each message, delivery of the messages and a host of other details involved in effectively communicating a project of this scope and magnitude to a global audience. Instead, the meeting was over in less than an hour and the plan was never brought up again.

After this meeting, I began to worry about the adequacy of the plan. I spent my lunch hour in the building cafeteria, going back over it and trying to figure out how I was going to possibly determine specific dates when I had received no frame of reference from Stephanie or anyone else. Halfway through lunch, Frank Watson joined me. Frank was an HR director before becoming director of public relations for the company and I knew him fairly well; or at least I thought I did. Like everyone else I worked with, I didn't know him at all. Of all the people I thought would stand up for what is right, it was him. It turned out to be a case of mistaken identity. The old saying is true. You can never really know anyone particularly when they are forced to make choices in a corrupt environment.

I showed him the plan and explained to him what Stephanie had said about inserting dates. He liked the plan as written and told me that leaders are not concerned with specific dates. They just want to know the long term vision and that there is an overall communications strategy in place. He confirmed what I thought as well and I did no further work on it. A month or so later, I sent an email to Stephanie requesting a meeting with her to discuss the dates she requested and she never responded to me.

Neither Rick nor Stephanie ever followed up with me to see whether I had inserted dates or not. They never cared about dates because they had no intention of ever referring to the plan again. I think their total dismissal of the plan had a bigger effect on me than I ever realized. That was when I really began to wonder what I was doing there. My job, as I understood it, was to help lead the communications efforts. My official title was North America Communications Lead. By totally disregarding the plan, ignoring my emails, not including me in on any of their meetings and not assigning me any work other than setting up their meetings; they sent me a clear message that my assistance would not be required.

Non-Responsiveness

For reasons I will explain later, I kept most of the emails I sent and received while on the project. Below are synopses of the emails I sent to Rick and/or Stephanie over the next two months concerning communications. I did not receive responses to any of these emails. Rick and Stephanie ignored them all.

Date	To	Email Text
5/03	Rick, Stephanie	Re: Approval of cost for bulletin boards to communicate team achievements
5/14	Rick, Stephanie	Re: Weekly calls with HR managers Rick could attend to keep company abreast of project
5/19	Rick	Re: Status and content of interviews with project teams and attaching summary of interviews and suggestions they had for improving communication and teamwork
5/28	Rick	Re: Creating a master spreadsheet for outstanding items discussed in Team Leader Meetings

The 5/19 email attached an action plan for improving engagement, teamwork and communication on the project based on the feedback I elicited from the members of all seven of the North American teams. (Attached as Appendix II) The work items generated by this action plan alone would have kept me very busy throughout the entire length of the project. A few months later, when Rick, Stephanie and their allies in management plotted to get me off the project; they lied by saying there were not enough activities for me. The whole time I was on the team, I kept reiterating to Rick that there was no project plan in place for our team's activities but my concerns fell on deaf ears. Even in the absence of a plan, if we had just sat down to discuss these emails and the kinds of actions they required, then there would never have been a lack of work for me (as if there ever was).

Rick and Stephanie had their own agenda. I am not sure about everything it entailed but they were determined not to acknowledge any work I did or opinion I held. They let all the ideas contained in the action plan sit in inaction while the motivation and engagement of the North American project teams deteriorated by the day. After leaving the company, I spent several years of my life obsessed with finding out the truth of why all these people acted as they did. Along with obsessing over it daily, I did a ton of research on bullying and mobbing. It was surprising to me how most cases of mobbing follow a set pattern. There is usually a critical incident that triggers it and I believe Rick's failure to take any action with regard to my May 19 email and action plan may have proved to be particularly troublesome for Stephanie and him in late August when the team survey came back with dismal feedback from the North American teams.

Under-work

Because of their non-responsiveness and failure to utilize me, I felt bored much of the time and took it upon myself to do my own research on change management. I spent a lot of time researching and printing articles from the Internet on change management, trying to learn as much as I could on the subject. I also researched what other companies were doing to create employee buy-in. I thought it would be a good idea to incorporate some of those ideas in our own communications strategy. I created an Excel spreadsheet and started entering some of the messages and ideas for possible use later on. After doing this day after day, knowing it was probably a fruitless effort anyway, I began to feel restless. I would go to the bathroom, walk outside for fresh air, get coffee, or just get up from my desk and walk around. I guess that's what I remember most. Getting up and walking around to break the tedium. It may even have been what motivated me to apply to the Master's Program in Education when I did. I had been thinking about returning to school for awhile, but there were some variables that did not make the decision as easy for me as it was in the past, the main one being how I was going to pay for it. Shortly after the downturn in June 2008, the company began cutting costs and tuition reimbursement was suspended for a time. I spoke to my father about what I wanted to do and he said that if I needed money to help out with tuition and books, he would be willing to pitch in. So, with that worry off my mind, I enrolled in the Master's of Education in Instructional Design Program at a local university.

Although I was feeling restless and bored, I wasn't sure if it was just me or if the other members of the team felt the same way. Along with Stephanie and Rick, there were three other people on the team besides myself: Brandon Acosta, Nicole Bennett and Vicky Dennis. Brandon and Vicky had similar responsibilities and worked together, more or less. Nicole was an enigma to me while she was on the project, mainly because she was rarely around. I sat next to her for several months when we both worked in HR and I liked her very much. Everyone liked Nicole. She worked in career development and it was a good fit for her because she was young, pretty and very personable. She made a very good first impression. We never saw much of her while she was on the team, however. Early on, her mother was diagnosed with cancer and she spent several weeks out of town taking care of her. By the end of my second month on the project, Nicole had joined one of the overseas teams and I didn't see or talk to her much at all after that. Therefore, it was quite surprising that the only email I received in my final days at the company came from her. But I will get to that later.

Vicky and Nicole had much more in common with each other than Vicky and I did and I think they would have gravitated toward one another if Nicole had been around more. I think what first brought Vicky and I together was the low opinion we both shared of Rick and Stephanie. I didn't know she felt the same way as I did about them until we had lunch together. We had talked briefly before this but never about our personal feelings on how the project was being run. This lunch was the first time I expressed to anyone, other than Rick, my frustration and disappointment with my new role. She had many of the same feelings, but when I mentioned to her that I was thinking about going to HR to discuss them, she strongly advised me against it. She had worked in HR at one of the field offices before relocating to the North American corporate office and I think she had some experience with how they addressed concerns that were brought to them.

However, it wasn't just human resources that Vicky had a problem with. There were certain other people in the company she didn't want me talking to either; particularly if they maintained a close working relationship with the home office overseas. Apparently there was a mindset held by Vicky and others within the company of which I was largely unaware. The company was a subsidiary of a larger, global company. Instead of looking at it as one unified company, many viewed our company as being a separate entity and were distrustful of the corporate home office overseas. Vicky and I always emailed back and forth in our meetings and during one of the meetings that Stephanie was conducting, Vicky wrote to me: "You know I really don't like the idea of them leading us in being deceptive of [the parent company] because if they find out, all of us will be held accountable." As with many of the things Vicky said and wrote, I had no idea what she meant but it might have had to do with this basic animosity and mistrust. It was a pretty dysfunctional relationship overall, particularly since it was a view held by some of the people in management. Vanessa Herron, the human resources manager I eventually went to with my concerns, mentioned to me that the parent company kept "spies" in every department.

I think Vicky viewed Adrian Bonavita as one of these spies. Adrian worked in implementing many of the company's change initiatives and was extremely knowledgeable about the subject and the company itself. At one point, I sent Rick an email regarding some of the ideas Lynette and I had for a communications plan specifically targeted to the change agents. The change agents were the employees at the locations who were designated to help us communicate the initiative locally and assist us with getting employees to accept and embrace the new system. I was upset by his response and forwarded his email to Vicky saying, "Someone needs to tell Rick there is no 'I' in team." Vicky never responded to this email, but the next day when I told her I was going to meet with Adrian to talk to him about change management, she told me to cancel because in her words, "He tells the home office everything." I was just getting ready to leave for the meeting when she said this but decided to take her advice and cancel.

This was another instance where I let someone else influence me to change my mind about something I had already decided to do. I cannot really give a good reason for why I followed her advice except to say that sometimes you just don't want to go against what your friends tell you to do. This was one of those times. I use the term 'friend' to describe my relationship with Vicky and maybe that is not the correct term to use. She was someone who knew exactly what I was talking about when I complained to her about Rick, which I did quite frequently. I sent her emails telling her the latest thing he said or did to me and would go cry on her shoulder when the frustration and anger would get to be too much to handle. Vicky always appeared to understand and she appeared like she was trying to offer words of comfort but her advice was always given in a very vague and cryptic fashion. I realized much later on it was because she was working both sides of the fence and she didn't want to do or say anything that threatened her own self interests and position.

It is very hard to write about what our relationship was like then because my dislike for her runs so deep now. I have concluded it was probably after our lunch meeting that she went to Rick and formed her alliance with Stephanie and Rick. It was then she began a fake friendship with me in order to gather information to help them. Everyone, and I do mean everyone, eventually turned against me and took some vicious actions to personally harm me and my mental health. Vicky betrayed my trust in unimaginable ways. It has been one of the hardest issues I have had to deal with and the only way I have been able to put it aside is by coming to an understanding of why she did what she did. Seeking the understanding of why she and all the others did what they did was what caused me to write this book.

The incident with Adrian happened on June 15. A lot happened that day, much of which was triggered by a June 14 email I sent to Rick regarding the change agent communications plan. I explained to Rick that I had put a lot of thought into coming up with a strategy we could use for the getting the employees talking in a positive way about the changes coming their way. I went through the vision I had and said that Lynette and I would be working on it together to fine tune the message. I finished by providing some ideas on print materials and other items we could utilize to educate and inspire the agents to spread the message, get feedback, and continually improve the change management process. Rick's weasel-worded response to this email became the final straw in what had become an impossible situation.

I am not sure why Rick chose to respond to my June 14 email regarding my ideas for the change agent communication strategy and not just disregard it as he had all the others, but I am glad he did because it provides a good illustration of the insidious way bullies use language to belittle their victims' talents and abilities. His email was meant for my eyes only and I got the message loud and clear. It read as follows:

> A couple of more comments about the change agent approach:
>
> 1. As mentioned in my other email in my perspective most of the change agents at the larger locations have been identified. We still need to finalize the others.
>
> 2. I want to start my communication with this larger group when I start visiting the locations the second half of the year. My main message will be their roles and responsibilities, help with identifying other agents for their sites, communication tools and the overall strategy for the change agents. Later in the year or early next year I will probably start monthly calls with this group to help ensure a consistent message and answer questions and give feedback on the feeling at the sites about the upcoming change.
>
> 3. When I start meeting with these individuals the second half of the year I do want to review the strategy with them so they have a good road map of where we are going with change agents (the handbook will help this) and then as you mention, Mary, provide a simple yet powerful message about their role and how we need their help. I know most of these individuals very well so I think it can be a very specific

and direct conversation.

4. In our teleconference yesterday, [the team leader overseas] mentioned they were working with an advertising group that was going to come up with a message and develop an internal campaign for the project. I think when we get feedback from this group we can incorporate your ideas below about posters, flyers [sic], etc. to make sure we don't mix campaigns and have a constant message and theme.

Thanks for your work on this, the internal campaign and change agent process will be keys to our success in change management.

Sometimes for a proper analysis to be done, you have to start at the end. In the last sentence of his email, Rick thanks me for all my work on the change agent strategy because the process will be key to achieving success in managing change. Someone reading this email who doesn't have the proper frame of reference might well conclude that he actually took some of my ideas into consideration and was planning on incorporating them in the change process. If I complained to anyone that Rick was totally disregarding and belittling my work based on this email alone, they would think I was being overly sensitive – or maybe even crazy. Victims can easily fall prey to these sorts of labels and need to be very careful and thoughtful in what they say about the bully and his behavior and how they choose to say it. It is very unfortunate, but a reality nonetheless, that the onus falls on the victim to remain calm and rational as she works out a strategy for resolution. The target of a bully must make it a priority to protect her reputation at all times because there is usually no one else – particularly HR – to help her out if she loses her cool over the unfairness of it all and does something stupid. Believe me, I know from experience. Your bully will push you and push you and as soon as you lash back in anger, they are ready to go running to the goon squad to have your head.

Unbeknownst to Lynette and me, Rick and Stephanie had already come up with a change agent strategy of their own without consulting Lynette or me. I can't say exactly what was in Rick's mind when he read my email, but I can imagine that there would have been a healthy dose of annoyance at my continued attempts to come up with ideas for communications. He had already made up his mind that he and Stephanie would be running this show without any assistance from me, hence his heavy use of *I* and *My* when he explains to me how it is all going to go down.

In the email I sent him, I had outlined a vision that Lynette and I had for delivering a message that the employees assigned as change agents could embrace and be happy about spreading, but he makes absolutely no mention of it. Nothing. Instead, he points out that an external marketing group will be coming up with the message and developing the campaign. The marketing firm was coming up with the visuals and theme for the system (product) itself. It is like advertising a car: "Razor – The Car of the Future for Forward Looking People." It is intended to conjure up a feeling about the car in your mind and gives the car company a common look and feel, but does not dictate what it will say in its materials about the car to targeted audiences like customers, employees, manufacturers, etc. We weren't proposing a campaign to him, we were proposing a *strategy* for helping the employee change agents be effective in bringing about change. Besides the fact that Rick was ignorant about marketing and communications, he was telling me in his "oh so nice way" that the advertising company knew much more than I did and he would limit my ideas *literally* to the use of posters, fliers, etc. in the campaign.

It might have been better if I had given myself a day or two to calm down and regroup. It wouldn't have changed what was happening on the project but it would have given me more clarity and focus with regard to what I wanted to tell HR when I went to them with my concerns. I must have spent the better part of the afternoon thinking about what Rick had written and how everything he said was in terms of "I" will do this and "I" plan on doing that. When something hits me the wrong way, that is usually what I do. I think about it for awhile and let it fester in my brain. That email definitely hit me the wrong way. It no doubt prompted me to get clarification from Rick on what his intentions were with regard to how the team would be utilized when we started traveling to the locations in the fall. His response once again irritated me and I immediately fired off the email to Vicky saying that someone needs to tell Rick there is no "I" in team.

I think it was a matter of minutes after reading his final email to me that I was headed to the other building to talk to Vanessa Herron. Vanessa was the go-to manager for most of the employees when they had an issue. She was always very approachable and I felt very comfortable going to her about my issues with the project. When I told Vanessa how totally defeated I felt and how confused I was about my role on the project, she told me I wasn't the only one who felt that way. Other project team members were telling her that they were sorry they ever signed up. She asked me if I wanted to speak directly to Steve Argon, the vice president of human resources or if I would prefer to have her speak to him. When I said I would prefer to have her speak to him, she asked me to put my concerns down in writing and she would discuss them with him. On June 16, I sent her the following email and attached the letter she requested which I have attached as an Appendix to this book:

> I have been working on the attached letter since we spoke yesterday and well into the night. I hope it adequately conveys what I am feeling without laying blame. I can honestly say that every person on this project wants it to succeed as passionately as I do and that is why I felt compelled to come to you.

In the attached letter, I expressed how honored I was to have been chosen for the project and how I and all the other team members were dedicated to its success. I told her, however, that I had strong concerns about the North American project leadership and the lack of a plan and overall strategy for implementing the new system. I also expressed how I thought the communications lacked creativity through the heavy use of Stephanie's templates. It was a two-and-a-half page, single-spaced letter that concluded with this paragraph:

> I have been told that things will get better once the roll-out begins in North America. That might be true and it might not. I don't know because no plan or strategy has been presented to us. I am not a manager and would not presume to tell a manager or leader how to lead his team. There are as many varieties of managing and leading as there are leaders themselves. Having said that, I do know from my own personal experience that some styles work and some styles don't. It is my belief that the top-down, consultant heavy style being used to lead this project is not working. Given the magnitude and scope of this project, I would just ask that someone review and analyze the situation to see if this is the best approach, or if there are alternative methods of working that will make this environment more team-oriented and make our people more productive.

I don't know if they took this letter as a formal complaint. It wasn't intended to be. When I wrote the letter, I tried very hard not to make it accusatory. I was unhappy and had tried working with Rick to improve the situation, but to no avail. When I wrote this letter, I was blissfully unaware that there was anything as horrendous as mobbing in the workplace. Mobbing was something done by out-of-control crowds in foreign streets; not in a safe, American working environment among colleagues who are encouraged to communicate face-to-face. Of course, I wasn't so naive as to not consider the possibility that I might make some people unhappy. I even voiced this concern in the beginning of the letter, but I had complete faith in the company's commitment to open communication. Maybe working in communications had worked against me. In everything I wrote for the company's publications, I always looked for an angle to tie the story to the company's values in a positive way. One of the company's core values was open communication and the leadership team often spoke of the need for transparency in all our interactions with one another. Unfortunately for me, I took their words to heart. I truly believed they would address my concerns fairly and impartially. There was no way I could have prepared myself for the onslaught headed my way.

Vanessa met with Steve the day after I sent the letter to her and shared with him what I had to say. I don't know what she told him, but I assumed she showed him the letter and they discussed it. When she followed up with me a week or so later to see how I was doing, I told her about a conversation I had with Stephanie at lunch that same week. We talked about the letter and Stephanie appeared to be very understanding. She told me how she wanted me to be happy working on the project but added, "Mary, don't you know you are never supposed to talk outside of a project?" I didn't know that and it bothered me a great deal afterward. I began to feel like I had done something wrong and I wanted to stop everything in its tracks before it got worse. As soon as I had the opportunity, I told Rick that everything was better and asked him not to say anything to Mike about the letter I wrote to HR. He said he had spoken to Mike briefly, but would assure him that everything had been resolved.

I felt good after talking to Stephanie at lunch. Even though her statement that I shouldn't talk outside the project made me nervous, the way she said it made me feel like it was for my benefit. Vicky was always clear as to the kind of person Stephanie was, but I went back and forth on it. She was just so pleasant to be around in social situations. When we had our team outings, I always gravitated toward her; or maybe she gravitated toward me. Rick always kept his distance at these functions and Vicky never attended them. I sat with Stephanie when we all went to a happy hour after work and she was on my team when we went bowling. Rick sat at another table at the bar and bowled on another team. I didn't notice it then, but these may have been the only two times I ever saw Stephanie and Rick apart from one another. They always went to lunch together, worked together and sat together at all the meetings. As I look back, it strikes me as strange that these were the only two instances I recall seeing the two of them apart, but it makes sense. I was probably the last person on earth Rick wanted to be around and I was totally unaware of it. I naively thought all was forgiven and we had all moved on. I have never been more wrong about anything in my life.

On one of the few occasions I did talk to Rick one-on-one after writing the letter, I suggested that our team have a meeting without Stephanie in attendance. I thought it would give us the opportunity to talk freely and openly with one another. Vicky told me she shared many of the same concerns I had and I thought it would be a good time for the team to hash some of them out. It would also give us a chance to come up with some of our own ideas for moving forward without the dominating presence of Stephanie. This is where a strong leader makes a difference. However, Rick was not a strong leader and he was not in there to lead. He wouldn't know how to even if he had the integrity to do so. He was there to cover up and obfuscate his real intentions with the help of his two new best friends – Nicole and Vicky.

The only way I can describe the meeting with Rick was sad. Brandon wasn't in attendance. This was probably due to intentional scheduling on Rick's part. If Rick had truly been interested in process improvement, he would have wanted all members of the team present. Brandon worked for a different subsidiary than the rest of us and was fairly independent. He worked directly with his own people for the most part and would have been an unknown quantity in a meeting that Rick wanted full control over. It was just Rick, Vicky, Nicole and me in attendance. Rick conducted it in his usual fashion and went around the table one-by-one asking us what we thought. Nicole and Vicky said they were fine with everything and didn't say anything else. By the time it got to me, I felt somewhat defeated as I once again mentioned putting a plan together and maybe even putting some ideas on the whiteboard. I don't recall much else that was said. They didn't take any of my suggestions and I think the meeting just whimpered to a close with nothing changed.

Vicky and Nicole were more than just mere bystanders. Neither one of them were managers, but they were both definitely on the managerial track in the sea of corruption that guided the policies of this company. In one of the books I read on handling bullies, the author emphasized the importance of building alliances in order to keep yourself from becoming isolated. Unfortunately, I could not follow his advice because everywhere I turned, the cards were already stacked against me. There is a very limited pool of alliances to be found in a company like this one if you do not want to compromise your integrity. Alliance building works in both directions, however, and Vicky and Nicole had both built their alliances with the right people to survive in this environment. Nicole was Vanessa Herron's best friend. Nicole knew the rules these people followed and consented to help them in exchange for the freedom to do as she pleased.

Vicky was a bird of a whole different variety. Like Rick, she is a personality type I would rather have never come to know. She did not like me from the start, which is now very clear. The thing that wasn't as apparent to me until recently is that I did not like her from the start either. I had worked with her on a article for the company magazine a short time before joining the project and it was a very contentious process. She sent me an initial draft and it was almost incoherent. It required so many edits and after going back and forth with her on it, she finally just quit responding to me. Kristine and I finally made the decision not to print it. Neither Vicky nor I ever talked about it after I joined the project, but I think it negatively impacted our feelings towards one another. We both decided to deny those feelings in order to pursue what we thought was in our own self interests. I thought I had an ally in her because she expressed the same dissatisfaction. I was willing to forget the article writing process and my feelings toward her to have a friend. I don't think she ever forgot the process because it allowed her to pretend to be a friend. I thought she was my friend, but deep down I knew something was wrong. She only did the essential things she needed to do to get information from me and only spent the time she needed to spend with me to be convincing. It makes me feel so stupid and dirty now. I should have paid more attention and not been so desperate to have a friend. She continued her pretense for months after I walked out when they were all afraid of getting sued and needed her to find out what my plans were. Unskilled and overpaid people will go to great lengths to keep what they've got. Bullies in power know this and will hold this power over their heads to get them to do what they want them to do.

In mid-July, all the North American teams traveled overseas for week-long meetings. During the trip, I had no idea that Vicky had already formed her alliance with Rick. As for me, I really thought we were becoming friends. It was fun having her with me. We ate meals together, worked out in the gym and went to the mall. We had a lot of free time to talk and get to know one another. We were both disillusioned with everything going on so we entertained each other while everyone else attended meetings. I had some work I was helping Lynette with, but Vicky had absolutely nothing to do. Neither one of us even knew why she was there. Stephanie and Rick had told her beforehand that she wouldn't be able to attend any of the meetings, but when she asked them if she could stay behind to work they insisted that she go. I really felt bad for her and tried to find things she could help me with.

Toward the end of the week, Rick held a team meeting. As usual, he went around the table and one-by-one had each of us tell him what we were working on. Vicky was the last one to speak. The boredom, anger and hurt of having to sit there by herself all week while everyone else attended the meetings (which she should have been in) just came to a head and she told Rick exactly what she thought of it. Then she began crying. Tears and all. She was very convincing. She told me later she spoke to him in private and worked everything out. I suspect they probably laughed about what a good job she did. Knowing what I know now and how Vicky knew everything about their strategy to get rid of me and the defenses they came up with in advance, I would not be shocked to learn that this whole scenario of not letting her attend the meetings was planned in advance. That way, she could sit next to me all week and form a common bond with me so that I would share personal information with her that they could use against me. The lack of empathy Vicky later displayed toward me makes me absolutely convinced that she would have no problem engaging in such treachery. Also, a very big reason why this has to be true is because Vicky is a black woman. Even Rick, as stupid and amoral as he is, would not be stupid enough to appear so discriminatory if Vicky was not cooperating with him. It would have put him in way too much danger of an accusation of discrimination. Knowing Vicky the way I do, she would have made this point quite clear if the story she was telling me was true. She would never have put up with such unfair treatment without taking revenge. In a moment of arrogance and extreme anger on my part later on when I became aware that Rick was not altogether stupid and was purposely undermining me, I even told her she was in the cat bird's seat because of this instance of "discrimination." I am sure she used this conversation to convince the executives she was helping to say that my motive was to sue the company. The thought that a "friend" actually liked her and was looking out for her never crossed her mind because in her mind, I was the enemy. It all gets so sick and twisted in corrupt environments and it is why victims are wary of seeking justice. They know their words and actions will be used against them and viewed by courts, juries and prosecutors as if they were spoken and done in rational and moral environments. My "friend" Vicky was setting me up every step of the way to accomplish this very goal.

Wrong Instructions And Unreasonable Deadlines

There was some discussion during this trip about the need for some change management materials Lynette's team needed for their upcoming meetings. As with all the other communications, nothing was said to me about preparing them and I just assumed that Stephanie and Rick would. I never stopped trying to make some sort of contribution though. I reviewed the change agent strategy he and Stephanie put together (before rejecting Lynette's and mine) and jotted down many questions and notes I had regarding it. I sent Rick an email asking if we could meet to go over it and begin detailing out the communications needed for the next phase of the project and update the plan. He said he would try to talk to me later, or touch base the next week. I shouldn't have been surprised when neither happened.

If I were to give Rick the benefit of the doubt, I would say he didn't follow up because he knew he wouldn't have anything to say. I no longer give Rick the benefit of the doubt. I now see him for exactly the man he is: a narcissist who despised me after I wrote the letter to HR. I should have seen it then, but I always look for the best in people. Rick had no 'best' to see. He and Stephanie toyed with me from the very beginning. They never had any intention of using me in the capacity to which I was assigned. They would have continued playing these games with me until they were able to make me transfer or quit, deriving great enjoyment from watching me deteriorate as I began to question myself at every turn. Their game eventually backfired on them but there was no need for them to squirm. After I wrote the letter to HR, they found out they had the power of the executive suite and its little minions to back them up. This was where the game got really fun for them. With his executive supporters in place, Rick could sit back and spin all kinds of lies and false accusations to get me out of the picture without any cost to him. It doesn't get any better than this for a bully like Rick.

We got back from the overseas trip on July 19 and I met with Stephanie sometime that week. Rick was not in attendance. She asked me to prepare the Change Management Handbook and a presentation that could be given to the change agents when the change management teams began visiting all the locations. It was a short meeting in which we never sat down. She said she would like me to prepare something similar to "Tell the Story" for the presentation and she gave me a one or two-page list of topics she wanted me to expand upon in the handbook. No further instruction was given or discussion had.

"Tell the Story" is the title I gave to the concept Lynette and I came up with for the change agent strategy that Rick rejected. The idea was that the change agents would be like apostles spreading a message. We needed to get the change agents to embrace the new system and believe it would be far superior to the current systems they were using. They, in turn, could spread that message out to their fellow employees. I felt strongly that the only way to get them speaking passionately about a system they were unsure about was to speak directly to their hearts, not to their heads. I was working on the *Tell the Story* presentation when I sent the email to Rick outlining our change agent proposal and he rejected it out-of-hand. The presentation was put on the shelf and nothing said about it until this impromptu meeting with Stephanie.

I probably spoke to Stephanie mid-week and on the following Monday I sent an email to Lynette telling her I wasn't expecting to prepare these materials, but would do my best to get something to her by week's end. I can't read what is in someone's mind, but Stephanie's subsequent actions led me to believe that she may not have expected me to get these materials done in the time allotted with the scant information she provided to me. One of the tactics bullies use is to provide you with little or no instruction for an assignment, hoping you'll get it all wrong. They also like to set deadlines they think you won't be able to meet. Stephanie did both in this instance.

She was not aware that I had been doing a lot of my own research on change management and was keeping both paper and computer files of the information I gathered. I used all this information, along with her outline and some of her slides, to prepare the handbook. It turned out to be quite good and she didn't make any substantive changes to it. She even told me I should write books. How ironic.

I sent a draft of the handbook to Stephanie on a Thursday and then started working on the presentation she requested. Early the next week, I sent an email to Rick saying I wanted to take a week of vacation the next week and he said that was fine as long as I got the handbook and Power Point finalized by the last week of the month. I worked on it the entire week so that I could get a final draft to both of them before I left on vacation. This also happened to be the week when the other teams were presenting their work to everyone on the project. I had to miss some of these meetings in order to complete the presentation and I heard secondhand from Vicky that Rick made a point of mentioning my absence. He was well aware that I was busy trying to finish up the handbook and presentation, so if he had a problem with me missing the meetings to meet his deadline, then he should have spoken to me directly. The fact is that Rick loved having me miss the meetings because it served his purposes. It gave him an opportunity to make me look bad in the eyes of all the project team members, most of whom had not worked with me before and were forming their impressions of me for the first time. I have no doubt that having Rick make it look like I didn't care about what they were doing forever damaged their opinion of me and probably made it very easy for them to dislike me and believe the lies being told about me.

Once I finished a draft of the Power Point presentation, I presented it to Liz Miller. Liz was hired for my position in communications while I was on the project. I had done some training with her and liked her immediately. I gave her the presentation as I would to an audience and she liked it very much. Other than tweaking the script, we didn't make any changes to it. After we finished, we talked for awhile about her professional background and she appeared to have quite a bit of experience with change management. She even gave me a couple of good suggestions from her own experience that I decided to incorporate in the handbook.

I sent a draft of the presentation to Rick and Stephanie before leaving on my vacation, if you can call it that. Actually, it turned out to be just what I needed. I set up a table in my living room, listened to music and did homework for school. My first class was a Javascript programming class. It was definitely nice being away from work. The difficulty was that I wasn't enjoying it with my husband. He walked out on me a couple of weeks earlier after we had a terrible argument in which I said some terrible things. We had fights earlier in our marriage, but he was always the one losing his temper and I was the one who would leave. He always came after me though and would make me talk it out with him. This time, however, he was the one who left and he never came back to talk it out.

3

THE MOBBING BEGINS

The Gruesome Twosome Show Their True Colors

When I got back from vacation, everything changed. There was nothing in my life before that could have prepared me for the next two weeks. Just two weeks. It doesn't take long to make a person think they are going crazy and then leave them with a self they no longer recognize, a mind unable to think and a life in total shambles. Sound melodramatic and over the top? Well that is exactly what my colleagues, managers and executives at this forward thinking, open communication, respect for others and value their opinions organization did to me when they ganged up on me. They didn't care about me or how their actions affected me. But for all other organizations out there who do care about the mental safety and not just the physical safety of their employees, then they better think long and hard about whether they have managers, supervisors and executives in place with the stamina, courage and character to do what is right at all times – especially when it's not easy.

I was expecting to come back to the same old, dull routine. It was anything but. While I was out, the results of a global team survey came back and the scores for the North American teams in the area of engagement were terrible. I had tabulated the results on the previous survey but was never shown the results of this survey. I hate to think of the possibility but it certainly makes me wonder whether Lynette knew what was being done to me. She was the one who asked me to tabulate the results for the previous survey in May but from this point on, I heard very little from her.

Not seeing the actual results of the survey this time around, all I had to go on was the dismay on Gary Boire's face when he met with all the North American teams to discuss the results. Gary was the global project leader. I never met Gary and was not familiar with his personality or temperament but he struck me as being genuinely concerned about the results and sincere in his desire to get to the bottom of them. I can't really say with any certainty whether I rolled my eyes at what I perceived at the time as his apparent lack of understanding for why the scores were so low because the reason was crystal clear to me. It was even more clear to Rick and Stephanie and I believe it was the catalyst for the mobbing against me.

> "**Mobbing**... is an impassioned, collective campaign by co-workers to exclude, punish, and humiliate a targeted worker. Initiated most often by a person in a position of power or influence, mobbing is a desperate urge to crush and eliminate the target. The urge travels through the workplace like a virus, infecting one person after another. The target comes to be viewed as absolutely abhorrent, with no redeeming qualities, outside the circle of acceptance and respectability, deserving only of contempt. As the campaign proceeds, a steadily larger range of hostile ploys and communications comes to be seen as legitimate ... Not infrequently, mobbing spelled the end of the target's career, marriage, health, and livelihood."[6]

I made a fatal mistake by dismissing Rick as simply an incompetent fool. He was no fool. He might have been inadequate for the job he was given to do but he was not about to let that stop him from retaining his prized spot in the food chain and getting the glory he felt was so rightfully his. In an email I wrote to Vicky many months later while still ignorant of her participation, I asked her why they didn't just send Rick back to the location he came from. He could have retained his same handsome salary, employment status and all the perks that went along with being a vice president in a large corporation. They could have made up a reasonable explanation for his departure that no one would have questioned and the project could have resumed with a person more qualified to assume his role. It would have been so easy. After getting me out of the way and becoming certain that I was not going to file a lawsuit, that is exactly what they did. I later heard that Rick was taken off the team and another person put in his position. I was completely disposable and once out of the way, I was out of mind too. Once they determined I wasn't going to sue, they decided to do the right thing – for them. They were cowards from top to bottom.

When I wrote the email to Vicky, I was still holding on to the delusion that I mattered. Sending him back to his previous position never even crossed their minds because the fact is, I didn't matter. They didn't care about me. They were a group of arrogant managers and executives who were accustomed to getting their own way and not being questioned about it. I became an object of contempt in their eyes when I had the audacity to question one of their own. The survey results may have been the catalyst for their ganging up on me, but it was the letter to HR that sealed my fate.

The Tuesday after returning to work from vacation, Stephanie asked me to meet with her to go over the presentation I prepared. It was just the two of us this time. Rick didn't attend. Even though she was a contractor employed by the company, Rick willingly and wholeheartedly handed authority over to her and she had become the equivalent of my boss. I sent all my work to her for approval and she was the one calling all the shots. At the time it seemed natural, but looking back now with a clear mind, it is clear to me how very dysfunctional this whole consultant-employee relationship really was.

It was just another piece of the very upside down world these two needed to create in order to accomplish their malicious goals. They were methodical in their planning. They had Stephanie do most of the harassing and bullying because she was female and not an employee. It was their way of protecting Rick. Stephanie could chase me off and I would be none the wiser of their motives. That plan went up in smoke as I will explain later, but it shows how evil, manipulative and disgusting every last one of them is. They planned to destroy me and my career almost from the day I started, if not sooner, when they found out I was assigned to lead the communications efforts they wanted full control over.

I could tell from the start of my meeting with Stephanie that she didn't like what I had prepared because she was not in her usual jovial mood. The presentation was in the style of "Tell the Story." This was what she requested in her original instructions to me, but I knew it was very different from the style to which she was accustomed. All the presentations she prepared relied heavily on bullet points. I incorporated too many graphics into this presentation for Stephanie's taste. That would have been a legitimate point for discussion, but she was not in this meeting to discuss or improve anything. She was there to attack. She began going through the slides one-by-one knit picking them apart. She would say, "This needs more explanation" or "You need to make this one more uniform so that we can use one presentation for all locations." I told her I could modify them easily enough to suit the requirements of each location, which is what I planned on doing anyway. When I referred her to the script for further explanation on a slide she questioned, I saw she didn't have the script with her. She just ignored what I said and went on to the next slide. It went on like this through the entire presentation, with her pointing out something wrong with a slide and me saying we really need the script. I left the meeting extremely angry. All that work, once again, was done for nothing. Her malicious motives were made perfectly clear by her failure to bring in the script. She was out for blood.

I went back to my desk and started all over again. I discarded everything I had done and threw together a presentation using slides from the change agent strategy she and Rick created, along with various other templates she had provided to us. I know it must have taken longer, but it seems like it took just a matter of minutes to prepare a new Power Point. I left a couple of the slides blank with the intention of having Rick and Stephanie complete them by putting in the activities for which the change agents would be responsible. These were the same activities that Rick and I would have discussed if he had ever bothered to meet with me when I requested him to during our trip in July. It was nothing complicated, but it was also not something I could come up with on my own. I needed Stephanie and Rick to talk to me and help me put together a list of activities that the change agents would be handling. Rick and Stephanie must have felt a huge sense of relief when the blank slides gave them a revised strategy for getting rid of me quickly before someone found out the bad survey results traced right back to them. No longer stuck with having to make vague references about my shoddy work and how I didn't understand anything, they could now accuse me specifically of being too stupid to grasp the change activities.

Rick's email response to the revised template presentation I put together was classic for a bully. His first sentence was, "I like the way the presentation is coming along," and then he went into his usual hot air repetition of what Stephanie told him. He knew this was a completely different presentation comprised of templates from Stephanie and yet he acted like it was just a few revisions that improved upon the original. What kind of person is this? How does one react to a response like this? As I thought about it, I became more and more upset and went to talk to Kristine about it.

Kristine is in her early 30's. Although I was much older than her,

her confidence, intelligence, and air of authority always made it very easy for me to view her as my boss. I trusted and respected Kristine and was always honest with her. I held on to the illusion for so long that they forced her to say and do the things she did. It was easier to believe she was an unwilling accomplice to the bullying and mobbing than to consider the possibility that she was a willing participant. It came to the point, however, that the only way to make sense of all the events that transpired was to conclude that Kristine was capable of doing just about any deceitful and dishonest thing she was asked to do.

Rick was not my supervisor as Vicky tried to make me believe when it was convenient for them to have me thinking that it was within his authority to force me off the project and into a job I didn't want. Kristine was my supervisor all along. Kristine was the one I went to about my problems with Rick. In one of our early conversations, she told me she spoke with Steve about what I was telling her about Rick, but the conversation ended abruptly when Steve responded to her with, "Rick is a vice president." She knew exactly what he was saying to her with that statement, as did I. Steve was her immediate supervisor. If he was unwilling to work with her and protect the company by resolving the situation to the satisfaction of all parties, then her options became limited. She could choose to act like a leader and risk being called a snitch like me by going over Steve's head or she could keep her mouth shut, her head low and do what she was told. Other than this one conversation with Steve, I am not aware that she ever spoke to anyone in an effort to resolve the problems I was having with Rick and Stephanie.

I have concluded that Kristine was immature in her role. Although she carried the title, I don't think she ever internalized her position as an HR director in a large corporation. She just didn't have the self-awareness required to effectively lead and back up the people within her charge. It took me quite awhile to quit blaming myself and to start placing the blame where it belonged. Having done so, I can say without hesitation that most of that blame lies with Kristine. She was my direct supervisor and continued to be my direct supervisor while I was on the project. When I was continually going to her crying and feeling completely frustrated and useless, she had a duty to get to the bottom of it. I was following the protocol the company had set up. I went to HR with concerns about the project itself. Even if the letter was colored by my immediate irritation with Rick over discounting my work, anyone reading that letter with a kernel of objectivity would have been able to discern that my concerns went far beyond disappointment with my own work. Add to that Vanessa's awareness that other team members were dissatisfied and it amounts to gross negligence for them to have completely discounted what I told Vanessa in person and in the letter she asked me to write.

All the times I went running to Kristine when Rick and Stephanie were treating me disrespectfully and making me feel stupid, she had an absolute responsibility to address my legitimate concerns. Going over Steve's head was not her only option. She could have gone to Mike. He was the project leader and the one responsible for its success. She could have gone to Gary, the global project leader. Hell, she could have gone to the CEO overseas. She knew him personally. The company had touted the importance of this project since its inception. Maybe she did. I don't know because she never answered me when I emailed her before and after leaving the company. She hides in the bushes just like all the rest of them. They should hide their heads in shame. This was not just about me or what they viewed as my petty concerns. The letter brought it out of the realm of local HR and they knew it. It is why their campaign against me became so vicious. They were hatching a plan to keep that letter from ever coming to light so that Rick would be protected and his competence never questioned. I can't help but conclude that Kristine knew fairly early on that their ultimate objective was my elimination because of the threat I posed and that would clearly explain why she did not look for other ways to help me. It would also explain Steve's failure to ever speak to me personally, particularly given the magnitude of the project and the fact that he was one of the members of the committee overseeing it.

After performing a cursory investigation in response to my letter so they could say one was performed and after reassigning the menial [and only] tasks assigned to me by Rick and Stephanie to Nicole and Vicky, all was said and done in their minds and Rick was free to deal with me however he chose. As long as they all stuck together, there was no reason why the letter would ever be seen by anyone outside their inner circle. They figured I would be gone as soon as I got fed up with Rick's tactics and they could take care of Nicole and Vicky by giving them new jobs for their silence. The team meeting I requested with them without Stephanie was a joke and I was the only one not in on it. Nicole and Vicky didn't say anything because that was a part of their deal.

I didn't know all this at the time and so naturally I ran to Kristine again after Stephanie ripped apart my work and Rick gave me his condescending feedback to the revised template presentation. I told Kristine exactly what Stephanie did and in the process of doing so, I told her that I had shown the presentation to Liz beforehand and she liked it. Kristine said that Liz had told her about seeing the presentation, but she didn't say anything further about their talk. I don't know what Liz told her, but I do know what she told me and I don't think Liz would have suddenly done a 180 and confirmed Rick and Stephanie's opinion of the presentation. A look in Kristine's eyes confirmed I was right. Just the same, she sent me right back to the lion's den to deal with Rick and Stephanie on my own.

I can't help but think how I would have reacted or what I would have done if I were in Kristine's shoes and one of my team members kept coming to me with problems similar to what I was expressing to her. I think I would have been confused, but then I would have been angry that she was being treated in such a disrespectful manner and I would have felt obligated to get to the bottom of it. Kristine just kept sending me back to them. She never spoke to Rick or Stephanie about any of it and took no affirmative action on my behalf. Her actions, or maybe I should say her lack of action on my behalf and her willingness to let herself become a lap dog for those with bigger titles reinforces how important it is for companies to use objective measures to promote people to managerial positions if they want to run ethical organizations. Tyrants who run unethical organizations use appointments, rather than a formal process, to advance the people they want advanced. There is no better way to get people to tow your own line than to appoint unqualified people to good paying positions. It makes them very amenable to doing what you want them to do because they know they can never earn their way into similar positions elsewhere. Kristine was from another country. She was taking English lessons when I began working for her. She was unable to write any of the communications herself and she either had me do it or she hired outside contractors. What she did have was a direct line to the CEO's office. He was from the same country as Kristine and had his own issues with writing and communicating to a foreign audience. Kristine provided him with the buffer he needed.

I remember Kristine was upset because an announcement about her promotion to the position of director of communications was not sent to everyone by email as was the custom for other people who were promoted. The excuse they gave was the economic downturn and the fact that they were cutting costs across the board. They felt it wouldn't send a good message. The real reason I think the announcement was not sent was because they knew how unqualified she was and they knew other people would know it. Many decisions are made and kept in secret by bullies and their cronies for fear of being exposed for the frauds they are.

Targets should take note of how people in their own organizations are getting promoted. Are they subject to review to make certain they have the requisite experience and skills to properly fulfill the duties of their new positions? Is the review process carried out objectively or has it been compromised to such an extent that it has become nothing more than a popularity contest, rather than an exercise in finding the most qualified people? How did the person who is bullying you get into his/her position? Doing this exercise may not help victims of workplace bullying in any concrete way, but it will serve to give them a more realistic picture of their circumstances.

After Kristine sent me back without doing anything, I was completely frustrated. Upon returning to my work area, I wrote an email to Rick and Stephanie saying, "I am at a total loss as to what my role in this process is. Could we meet this afternoon to discuss?" Rick responded with, "Sure, how about 1:30 pm." What happened in this meeting began to show me just how awful these two people are. It is hard to think or write about them. Maybe that is why I have deflected so much of my anger towards everyone else involved and have tended not to think about the two of them so much. I still don't want to face the fact that people like them exist, but they do and they are thriving in the management circles of many corporate and governmental organizations.

Like all of our other meetings, Stephanie took the reins and set the tone. Rick just sat back and followed her cue, as he always did. I so vividly recollect what she said to me when I expressed concern over presenting materials that I had not personally had a hand in preparing. I was referring to the second Power Point presentation I threw together with her company's templates. When I told her I would need more details on the change agent network process before I attempted to explain it to the change agents at the locations, she looked at me as if we had gone over it a hundred times before and I was just not getting it. Then with a sincere expression of disbelief she asked me, "Don't you understand the road map I provided to you?"

Stephanie's question about the road map was pretty much off the wall in the context of this meeting. I was asking for details about the change agent process, as I had been since the trip in July. This was not rocket science. It was not even strategy. It was simply a matter of sitting down together and talking about the kinds of activities that would be required of the change agents at each stage of the process. Referring me to the road map was ludicrous. The road map was a one-page pamphlet that basically contained an illustration of the overall time line of the project phases. It had nothing to do with the specific change management activities that would be required of either the change agents or of our team. I should say what was left of our team. By this time, Vicky had announced she was leaving and Nicole had already transferred to a different area of the project. Other than me, Brandon was the only other team member left.

It was deja vu all over again. I am not sure if 'sincere' is the correct word to use because she was not sincere. From that first meeting I had with her in the beginning of the project she was never sincere in her interactions with me. But the look and feel of sincerity was her ace in the hole. It is why I was always on the fence with her. She was always the pleasant and cheerful one but now her armor of sincerity was cracking. She was becoming increasingly irritated with me and was not displaying the good humor and joviality that had become her trademark in these meetings. I suspect it was because she and Rick were becoming desperate and the time for good humor was over. They had to figure out a way to get me off the project (and with any luck, out of the company) before the corporate office that Vicky was so fearful of found out what they did and how their flagrant disregard for the integrity of the software implementation could have long-standing repercussions for the company in terms of costs, productivity, profitability and employee engagement.

Stephanie knew exactly what she was doing by referring me to the one-page pamphlet. Providing details to his target is not in a bully's DNA. He wants to keep everything vague with his victim so that he can say things like, "She has an inability to grasp the simplest concepts;" "She never seems to know what is going on;" "She shows no willingness to learn;" and "She can't even complete the simplest assignments we give her." If he says these kinds of things often enough and to the right people, the word begins to spread and people start changing their opinion of the target. That is why mobbing is likened to a virus that travels through the workplace, infecting one person after another. This is what Rick did to me and I was powerless to stop it. It was all going on behind the scenes. I tried to find out on a couple of occasions what he was saying about me but no one would talk to me. My last week there, I was not receiving any work, emails or telephone calls. No one came by to see me and in one email I sent to Kristine, I pathetically put in the subject line: "Please talk to me." I was feeling so sad, confused and alone and she had always been the one who made things better. Her calculated and cold response to this plea was how everyone would be responding to me from here on out – that is, if they responded to me at all. She tells me, "Mary, please come by and let's talk. I was waiting for you in our staff meeting and you didn't show up. I thought we had things clear after our meeting with Rick." When I explain the utter humiliation I was subjected to during and after the meeting she is referring to with Rick, you will understand why I didn't take her up on her offer to "let's talk."

Self-preservation can make people take desperate actions. Even though I now know the kind of person Rick is and I know he must have been denigrating me to anyone who would listen, there was something much more sinister at play here and people far smarter than Rick were getting worried. Every time I think back on that time it feels like one of those movies where the character gets caught up in a rushing river and starts grabbing at tree limbs, rocks – anything to keep from heading down the falls. Things were happening all around me and about me that didn't make any sense at all. The current kept getting stronger and stronger as I was being forcibly pushed into a job I was undeserving of and ultimately out of the company I loved because of Rick's lies. As unbelievable as this may sound, no one ever bothered to speak to me about any of it.

I don't even know how to write about this next phase. It is hard to think that I became viewed as absolutely abhorrent with no redeeming qualities. I have spent my life trying to be good and do the right thing. I thought I was doing the right thing when I wrote the letter to HR. Even though Vicky didn't agree with it, I never thought she and my other colleagues would despise me for it. There was apparently nothing that was beyond the pale in their treatment of me. That's what you do to a snitch who breaks the rules of the club. Most clubs usually have a leader and this one was no exception. The orchestrated campaign to isolate, humiliate, threaten and ultimately expel me from the company could not have been waged with such precision had it not been for someone at the top signing off on it. In the words of Jack Earl, "If the employer of 100 men be himself evil, he is to a great extent the evil environment of those 100 men. The curse of his evil is upon them."[7]

My last weekend there, I called Ed Odom, the general counsel and chief ethics officer I originally worked for when I joined the company, in a desperate attempt to stop this campaign and try to save my job. I get into the details of this conversation later on, but his initial words to me indicated to me that he was already aware of the situation and his parting words to me indicated that he didn't care. If Ed was aware of the situation, so was the charmer of a CEO at the top. Ed was his good buddy and sat in the office next to him. He wouldn't have kept our conversation from him.

Their elaborate plan could have been pulled off without a hitch if they hadn't miscalculated Rick's desire to get back at me all costs. Rick cared as much about his executive supporters as he did about me – not at all. They put their integrity, professional responsibility, reputations, sense of fairness, honesty and values on the line to protect an insecure, cowardly and manipulative bully.

After writing the letter to HR and then asking Rick not to talk to Mike about it because of the conversation I had with Stephanie, I thought the entire matter was done and settled. For Rick, I think it was anything but settled. That was when the war really began for him. When I put myself in Rick's shoes - knowing how much he prized the authority of his position and did not like to have it questioned – I can't help but conclude that my letter to HR must have had his blood boiling. It might have gotten a lot of people's blood boiling if they were in his place. I did not pull any punches in the letter. I knew that I could have been more diplomatic in how I voiced my concerns, but I made the conscious decision to be as clear as possible about what I saw as problems.

Rick's insecurities could not have possibly allowed him to take the letter in the manner in which it was intended. I kept making a point in the letter that my intention was not to attack anyone or lay blame at anyone's feet. However, there were actions being taken by Rick and Mike that I did not agree with and I did not feel served the best interests of the project or the teams. I would not have been honest with myself if I failed to address some of those concerns, but I wonder as I sit here today how I would have felt if I had been in Rick's shoes. It is likely that I too would have focused on the parts of the letter specifically about me. However, that is where all similarities between us end.

Although I never personally spoke to Steve, I know that Steve met with Rick to talk about the letter because Vicky told me that the subject of headcount came up in their meeting. I am certain that headcount largely influenced the strategy that was used for getting rid of me. Headcount is simply the number of people in an organization. Since Kristine made the decision to hire someone for my position in communications, there was no way I could return to communications because that would have required hiring an additional person to take my place on the project. Steve couldn't do that.

For once, I may have made Rick leave a meeting angry instead of the other way around. Unlike me, Rick couldn't show his anger after his meeting with Steve. He had to come across as the understanding team leader who had listened to my concerns and taken them to heart. All that resentment and disgust for me had to be held in check until the moment was right to let it all out. He was always pleasant enough in our meetings, but we didn't socialize or talk to one another much after the letter to HR. That duty was handed over to Stephanie. It suited me fine because Stephanie was fun to be around. That is, until the last few weeks I was there and she and Rick were having to contend with the mess they had created for themselves. The lioness who had been slowly and patiently helping Rick stalk his prey looking for just the right time to pounce, could no longer wait. Circumstances required my immediate termination.

If they could somehow get me out of the picture, they would have a good chance of gaining back some of the ground they lost. Maybe they could even incorporate some of the ideas from the action plan I sent them in May and make them their own. I don't think it was a coincidence that on my second-to-last day there, I received an email from Lynette, with a cc to Stephanie, providing her with specs on the bulletin boards I suggested using in that action plan. Bullies like to steal work and claim it as their own. I wonder how much of my other work and research they incorporated as their own. After all, once the snitch is gone it is like she never existed at all.

What would otherwise would have continued as bullying by Rick and Stephanie quickly escalated into a situation where the powers of the executive office were garnered against me. In mobbing cases, rumors, lies and innuendo are all used to discredit the victim's character and dehumanize her in everyone's eyes. By turning her into an object of scorn, the perpetrators' consciences remain clear and allow them to do anything they need to do to get rid of the "troublemaker." This is a term Vanessa used right after I wrote the letter to HR, when she said to me that she told Steve I was not one. Her opinion changed at some point because when I went to her in tears my last day, she told me there was nothing HR could do unless I filed a complaint.

Stephanie left the room shortly after directing me to the pamphlet in my August 26 meeting with Rick and her. True to form, she did not provide any details about the change activities and left the meeting shortly after it started claiming she had a telephone conference she had to attend. In an email I wrote to Kristine right after the meeting, I describe the ensuing conversation with Rick as follows:

> It gave me an opportunity to talk to Rick one-on-one. I told him how I need to have more direction and details, so that I don't continue to do work that just gets re-done. I think he understands my frustration and told me to come to him any time I have questions or concerns. Maybe it is all just part of this process … I don't know anymore.
>
> Anyway, they said that I would be giving the change agent presentation and I expressed some of my concerns and discomfort about giving a presentation on something I just copied and pasted and is a subject that I am not real familiar with. [the template presentation I threw together after they rejected mine out-of-hand] Rick said this process is new to all of us, but reassured me that he and Stephanie would be there to help answer any questions. When I tried to get more specifics on the process, Stephanie was not real anxious to volunteer any insight or templates. Instead, she asked me if I understood the road map she provided. I told her I understood, but the devil is in the details. She left soon after.

Rick and I decided in our one-one-one discussion that I should go through the presentation and other materials and present Stephanie with a detailed list of questions that I would like answered. I will start doing that and see how it goes.

I gave Stephanie and Rick just what they needed in this August 26 meeting. What relief they must have felt when I reinforced their strategy by saying I needed to have more direction and details and was uneasy about giving a presentation on something I just copied and pasted and was a subject I was not real familiar with. My phraseology of needing more direction must have been so good that they cc'd others on it, or maybe they even discussed in one of their strategy sessions to plot my demise. When I told Vicky I believed that our emails were being monitored, Vicky began giving me typed or handwritten notes rather than sending me emails. In one of these letters, she coincidentally used the same phraseology when she told me a move to HR might be good for me because Kristine could provide me with more direction.

Putting down in writing that I told Rick I needed more direction and details so that I didn't continue re-doing work was such a mistake on my part. It gave credence to their claims that I was stupid and slow to catch on. The fact of the matter is that they hadn't given me anything to go on. Stephanie and Rick purposely withheld all information and actively worked against me so that I would be unsuccessful in my job. They were setting me up for failure. I was being kind in my approach with Rick and it was reflected in that email. I was always kind. Evil people with evil motives will use your kindness against you. You don't want to quit being kind, but you also can't let it work against you when dealing with ruthless people. My advice to other targets is to put your kindness on the back burner for awhile and be smart. Double check every email communication you write to make sure it clearly says what you want it to say without giving your bully ammunition to use against you. I just can't emphasize this enough. As soon as you suspect that you are being sabotaged, the guns need to come out. You cannot give an inch. Just remember that you are smarter than the SOB who is doing this to you. Keep up your stamina, swim with the current and fight back smarter, not harder. What I should have said in the email is that Stephanie and Rick continue to stonewall me whenever I request information from them that I need as the communications lead on this project. I should have pushed Kristine to do something about the untenable situation since she was my boss and that was her job.

After the meeting on the change activities, it was clear I was being jerked around by Rick and Stephanie. I never prepared the questions for Stephanie as Rick suggested. The whole thing was getting totally ridiculous and I was totally fed up with them, the boredom of having nothing to do and the stress of trying to work with them and Kristine to change the absurd situation. I should have been anything but bored at this stage in the process. Here we were two short on the team and would very soon be traveling to all the locations to introduce them to the project and let them know what their roles would be in ensuring its success. I should have been knee-deep in preparation and worrying about how I was going to get it all done. Instead, I was sitting at my desk wondering what I could do to occupy my time.

This is absolutely deadly for someone like me. I have to be doing something. To compensate, I would go to the restroom, get coffee or just sit outside by the fountain to think. Once again, hindsight is 20/20. My advice to anyone who is being bullied with a strategy of being given too little or no work to do is to do anything to make yourself look busy. Don't let other people think your bully is right when he says things like, "She doesn't want to learn anything or take on new responsibilities." Your natural inclination will be to throw it in their faces because you know they are purposely doing it. That was my intent when I sat at my desk reading a book my last week there. This is the time, however, you should be pulling together all your inner resources to fight fire with fire. Until you have a viable solution, appearances are all that matter. You need to do whatever you can to protect your reputation for being a good worker as much as is possible. Do not let your bully define you.

I simply gave up and in an email to Kristine on August 31, I wrote, " I want off this project. I am not needed and feel totally useless." Kristine was so relieved at receiving this email that she responded with, "Hahaha." Do you want to come by?" I thought this meant she was happy at the thought of having me back on her team. Boy, was I out in left field with that assumption. She was anything but happy with me or with having me back on her team. When I talked to her that afternoon, she said she would talk to Steve about having me come back to HR. If it was ever her intent to talk to him, she never got the opportunity because Rick and Stephanie had plans of their own. Things began moving very quickly from here on out.

My last day at work was Friday, September 10, less than two weeks after this "ha, ha" email from Kristine. As I go over the events of these last days, this email marks the first in series of errors (or divine interventions) that prevented these people from achieving what they ultimately wanted to do to me. On Wednesday, September 1 (the day after the ha,ha,ha email from Kristine) Rick came by my desk and said he wanted to talk. We went into the large conference room where we always held our team meetings. I sat down at the conference table and he stood at the other end of the table. After he started in about how I didn't understand the change activities, I again tried telling him that we never discussed the activities, there was no plan in place and Stephanie seemed to be running the show. He immediately took issue with my last statement and firmly reminded me that he was in charge. His ego was so huge he took issue with the fact that I pointed out their designated hit man for the harassment was taking over. He was as stupid as I thought. I think he was expecting me to defend myself against his accusations in my usual fashion and he was taken completely off guard when I just looked down at the table and told him I would talk to Steve about getting off the project. He practically jumped out of his skin when I said that and quickly replied, "NO. Don't talk to Steve. I'll talk to Mike." I said "fine" and got up and left the room.

I went straight to Vicky's desk to tell her what Rick had just had the nerve to say to me and she told me, "At least you weren't insubordinate to him." This is not the kind of response one would expect from a friend but given the kind of 'friend' Vicky was, it must be viewed in the context of all the other events that were rapidly occurring in succession. I think this is where Vicky became a key player. The puppet master pulling the strings and his little minions didn't like the emotional emails I was writing, which touched on the liability they created for themselves by protecting their pal, Rick. They needed my "good friend" Vicky to coddle me and downplay my complaints. Too bad they didn't know Vicky the way I have come to know Vicky. She is one of those people who loves being in the know and she loves for other people to know she knows everything. Put simply, she couldn't keep her mouth shut. Not even to me. Vicky had a boatload of information and she needed to get it out. She couldn't tell me anything outright, so she played a little game of cat and mouse where she would feed me tiny little morsels of information that didn't make sense to me, but it relieved her need to tell. Two of these little nuggets of information lingered in the back of my mind for the longest time but once I put a time line together almost two years later, they were the keys that unlocked the evil of these people and the extremes they were willing to go to destroy my life. Headcount was one of these little nuggets and the other was something she told me about the "work plan." Keep these two concepts in mind as I go through the events of September 1 - 10. As

I think and write about the events that took place over those ten days, I keep wanting to qualify everything with "I didn't know then" or "If I had known then." It doesn't serve any purpose for me to do that or for any victim of bullying and mobbing to do that to themselves. Bullying and mobbing are deceitful, evil behaviors that take place in the dark. They were doing all they could behind the scenes to get me off the project and out of the company as quickly as possible. I had no idea what was happening to me, which is why my world became a surreal place where nothing made sense. I felt like I was going crazy. In actuality, I was the only sane one in the bunch. They had all gone too deep in their own deceptions, cover-ups and lies to ever come out of it looking like they acted rationally in any sense of the word.

I cannot emphasize this enough. Bullying and mobbing victims must always remain conscious of the fact they are in irrational environments controlled by people whose minds have been corrupted. They must never let the rot enter their own minds. In these corrupt environments, a person who has been targeted has been targeted for destruction. There is no reasoning your way out of the situation. The power imbalance puts a target in a non-winnable position. The best you can do if you want to save your career and financial viability is to get out on your own terms before they are able to completely destroy your well-being and chances for recovery. If you are at the top of the hierarchy, you do it by accepting the offer to resign and working out a beneficial exit package on your way out the door. For a target on the bottom row of the hierarchy, it is not quite so pleasant. It may mean leaving the job you absolutely love. For a spouse, it may mean getting out. For a student, it may mean transferring to another school. It is unfair. It is unjust. It is completely messed up but it is reality for as long as we allow these human power imbalances to exist. You can try fighting within the system but it will be a futile effort because the people who are assigned to help you, like my manager, will be as compromised as she was. It is simply not in their best interests to help you when they have their bosses and colleagues telling them you are the troublemaker who needs to go.

For the sake of educating other victims and making bystanders and enablers of bullying more aware of the personal destruction they cause, I will tell my story from this point forward as it happened, with as little commentary and "what ifs" as possible.

After talking to Vicky about my meeting with Rick, I ran straight to Kristine's cubicle to tell her about Rick's false accusation. I was crying and when she saw how upset I was, she wanted to go to a conference room where we could talk in private. As we walked down the hall together, she asked me about Vicky and when I told her that Vicky was transferring to a different department and job, Kristine replied, "At least she did it the smart way." Simply unbelievable. What kind of statement is that for a director of a global corporation whose team member is experiencing such unfairness to make? Not only does it prove she had direct knowledge of the hostile environment Rick was creating, it also shows me what an incompetent, callous and ineffectual manager she was. Too bad for me.

When we got to the conference room, we stopped at the door and never even sat down. Kristine told me she didn't have a chance to talk to Steve as we had discussed when I went to her the previous day after her ha, ha email. When I told her what Rick said, she once again did nothing to help me. Instead, she told me I was "dealing with power" and that I needed to go back and apologize to Rick - the man who had just blatantly lied to me and told me not to go to Steve.

I am surprised that Kristine would let the cat out of the bag like that and openly tell me it was power I was dealing with. I think it is because she was so inexperienced and uneducated about HR and legal issues. She was appointed to her position for reasons other than experience and knowledge. She didn't earn the title. Even worse for me is that she was weak in terms of her own character and value system. She never once asked to see the change management handbook I authored or the presentation that Stephanie tore apart in order to make a determination of her own about whether or not I understood the activities as Rick was alleging. Kristine let herself become a pawn in a very nasty game being carried out by all the power players pulling her strings. There were avenues she could have pursued to help me but she chose not to. She was in it to protect herself.

I went back to the work area as she told me to but I had absolutely no intention of apologizing to Rick. Later that day, Mike sent me a meeting notice to talk about the change management activities. I wasn't sure what he meant by that, but I assumed Rick had run straight to him after our confrontation in the conference room. I sent an email to Kristine to tell her that Mike wanted to talk to me and although she wanted me to keep her advised of what he said, she never offered to join us.

Mike was the North American project leader, but other than arranging a few lunches and team outings at his request, we never really talked much. I always got the feeling he didn't like me or feel very comfortable around me, so I was rather surprised at how easy it was to talk to him about my problems with Rick and Stephanie. But then again, I think it would have been easy to talk to anyone who showed the least bit of interest in what I had to say. After all, as I later realized, it was his job to make me feel relieved and comfortable so I would open up to him and give him as much information as possible before they canned me. It was in this meeting that their story changed from "not understanding the change activities" to "a lack of activities." No doubt this change in stories was made due to the email I sent to Kristine about feeling useless. Actually it worked to their advantage to change their story because then they could have the HR manager meet with me first thing on the following Monday to tell me I was no longer needed. Monday was the day Vanessa Herron used for terminations. I am sure Ed advised them that there would be no liability on their part if I filed a lawsuit after my termination because they could claim no one knew of Rick and Stephanie's harassment since I never went to anyone in HR about it. Of course Ed was not aware of how stupid Kristine was in telling me that Vicky did it the smart way. All Ed knew is that I live in an at-will employment state where employees can be laid off at the will of the employer without liability. Although I was in a couple of protected classes, here they had documentation in my own words that there was not enough work for me. If not for Rick ruining it for them with another meeting which I will get into, they would have gotten away with everything free and clear.

Mike started his meeting with me by saying they were planning on sending me back to HR due to a lack of activities for me on the project. When Mike asked me what I thought, I told him everything I had been telling Rick since I first started on the project; specifically that there was no plan in place. I remember using the analogy of trying to write a book without an outline, not realizing how true that comparison was. How can they determine there is a lack [or a misunderstanding] of activities without first knowing what the activities are? I also told him how Rick and Stephanie were treating me and how they made me feel stupid. I don't remember everything he said in reply because I focused and held on to his words when he said to me, "You're right. We've failed miserably." The sense of relief I felt was immediate. Finally, there was someone who was validating what I knew to be true and he was actually going to take steps to resolve the situation. Now I realize how deliberate those words were. They guaranteed no visit to Steve Argon, the HR vice president, before Monday.

We continued talking. He was interested in what Lynette's team leader was doing to foster teamwork and he seemed genuinely interested in what I had to say. It was so refreshing and so different from my experience with Kristine, Rick and Stephanie. As we concluded our meeting, he said he would give Rick some team coaching and things would be different. Then as we stood up and headed out the door, I told him how much I wanted to work with Vicky, Nicole and Brandon, not mentioning Rick or Stephanie. It was very Freudian, but it ended up not mattering anyway.

Right after talking to Mike, I sent an email to Kristine telling her that my conversation with him went great. I suggested we go to lunch the next week because by then I would have a better idea of how everything was proceeding with Rick, Stephanie and the work. We never did go to lunch and she never came by my work area. Not then, not ever.

My utter joy at the possibility of finally having a resolution was short-lived. Actually, it lasted all of six hours. Rick came by my desk late in the afternoon and asked to speak with me. This meeting needed to take place in complete secrecy where it would be his word against mine. He took me into a small, windowless conference room where there was just a small table between the two of us. He told me he met with Kristine earlier in the day and they decided that I would work with her while the change activities were going on because, according to him, I did not understand them.

I wasn't aware of all the machinations going on behind the scenes when I was looking in the face of evil in that small, windowless room with Rick. I was sitting there innocently thinking Rick was telling me this because he hadn't yet had a chance to talk to Mike. I begin telling him very calmly and nicely how I explained to Mike that there was no plan in place as to the kinds of activities that would be required and they need to be spelled out and discussed before I can have an understanding of them. His thin little lips began to quiver and his miserable little face became as distorted as his mind when he came back at me with his usual nonsense that there is a learning curve for all of us. That was his favorite line whenever I brought up any idea or concern. He said it with a smile, but it was a contorted, uncomfortable smile that told me all I needed to know. I hated him at that moment. Up until that point, there was always the possibility that he was just stupid and was covering it up by acting authoritarian and giving non-responses that sounded like responses because he didn't have the answers. Now I knew. If he was stupid, he was also evil. He was acting purposefully and maliciously toward me and I felt it clearly in that small room as I sat across from him looking in the empty set of eyes he hid behind the horn rimmed glasses. Whether he had talked to Mike or not, it didn't matter. I knew there was no point in continuing. When he asked me if I had anything further to say, I just said "no."

Rick knew how well protected he was when he repeated his false allegation in the small windowless room, hoping it would put me over the top since I tend to be an emotional kind of girl anyway. Undoubtedly, he was hoping that I would start yelling at him or do something else that would justify my immediate dismissal. How surprised he was when I calmly repeated what I told Mike in our meeting, in a further attempt to make him understand that you cannot have a misunderstanding of activities that were never discussed in the first place.

Rick was correct in his assessment that I am an emotional kind of girl. I think he loved that quality of mine because he could use it to his advantage to get me to react emotionally to his lies and do something that was not in my best interest. That's what Vicky meant with her insubordination comment. She knew this was their strategy and she played right along.

I fired off an email to her immediately after this meeting with Rick. Our exchange is shown below:

Me:
I had four whole hours during which I felt hopeful and then I spoke with Rick. It's all an illusion.

Vicky:

Yep. So now you have to be part of that illusion and let go of reason and ration. Let go of your high expectation, smile, when you do anything ask for Stephanie's input (even if you want to throw up), smile some more and then concentrate on your homework. You expect more from yourself then they expect from you.

Me:

No. I've been 'demoted.' While the "change activities," which I don't have a 'good understanding' of (which is what he actually had the nerve to say to me) are going on, I will work with Kristine. Then, if some activities arise that they may need my help on, they will call me back.

Vicky:

Wow. Hum....interesting.
No one got a pay increase for coming to the project so demotion is a strong word.
It may not be a bad idea to have Eleana as a buffer as I am sure she would give you clearer direction. Its just the tone makes it again as if the problem lies only with you. Not cool.

Me:

As usual, you're right. Thanks for working with me through my venting.

———————

I would have loved to have been a fly on that wall when Vicky showed them all the email regarding my feelings about being demoted. I was right in viewing it as a demotion and they knew it. They must have begun feeling some regret over their decision to protect Rick at all costs. He was proving to be not only an harasser, but an ingrate of one at that. He was creating liability for them by the minute, but they were in way too far over their heads to ever be able to back out gracefully.

It was Vicky's job to calm me down when I would point out the obvious. She could sound so casual as she lied to me. Actually, I remember being very upset over this email exchange. I wasn't as peeved over her inadequate definition of demotion as I was with her saying that the tone of Rick's words made it sound like the problem lies only with me. She was thereby telling me that I was part of the problem. I wasn't part of the problem but even if I was, who wants a friend to so halfheartedly support them? But then again, she was all I had so I let it slide without saying anything to her. I was always praising her and telling her she was right even when she wasn't. It was my way of being nice, but it was the wrong thing to do. It is just as wrong as telling a lie to protect yourself because in both instances what is being said is false. I think the goal should always be truth. That is the only way to motivate people and get them to reach their full potential. We do ourselves and others a disservice by using superficiality and false sentiments in trying to build self-esteem and make people feel good about themselves. Ultimately, the only way a person truly feels good about themselves is when they create a self worth esteeming. False sentimentality and appearances that seem to rule our present world create the illusion that we are good people when we are anything but. Everyone in my workplace felt so good about themselves and their actions – and I include myself in that category. We are so lost in the illusion and we have not given ourselves a way out because our strong egos go into overtime protecting our self images at all costs. We are not taught how to examine ourselves honestly.

All the people involved thought I was an ignorant low level employee. They thought they could feed me false information and I would just accept it because I didn't know any better. They were confident they could string me along and calm me down enough so that I wouldn't go to HR to file a complaint.

At the core of this Machiavellian nightmare was the strategy of plausible deniability – a favorite of politicians and other corrupt and cowardly types who want to get around the law to accomplish their personal agendas. Truth must be destroyed for the illusion to win. This group of well-educated, well-paid and well-connected professionals spent a couple of weeks of their lives coming up with lie after lie and manipulation after manipulation without a single one of them bringing truth and rationality to bear on the situation. In such an environment (if there are laws on the book) as there were with me, then they must figure out a way to get around those laws in a manner that does not make them look like criminals or otherwise tarnish their images. That is what plausible deniability does. It allows you to break the law while setting up the situation in a way that allows you to deny that you broke the law. Not only that, if you are crazy enough to reason your way around the law in this manner while thinking that this reasoning is in any way whatsoever a rational and sane way to conduct one's affairs, then you will absolutely have no problem in accusing the victims of your crimes of being the crazy and guilty ones.

Bullies and the mob rely on the illusion. They cannot get away with their atrocious behaviors if other people are condemning them. They must turn good into evil and evil into good to accomplish their goals. This simple truth is so logical and clear to me now. When you band together to protect a buddy who has done something wrong, then you must create the illusion that your buddy is the rational and good one while his victim is the crazy one out for revenge. It is the lifeblood of the legal defense system and countless lives have been destroyed by it while the abusers have survived and thrived in the systems and organizations that protect them.

While reading about bullying and mobbing and doing a lot of research on Adolf Hitler (arguably the biggest bully in history) I came across the story of Raoul Wallenberg, a man who saved thousands of Jewish Hungarians during WWII. At a very low moment during the war, he told a Swedish Red Cross worker: "Even while we speak, somewhere, someone else is being murdered by the

Arrow Cross . . . Laws no longer exist here; anything can happen. Sometimes one can't get from one street to the next . . . Anyway, reality doesn't matter any longer, illusion does."[8] Illusion will always be what matters when the guilty are caught in their wrongdoing and are trying to get away with it. It is no wonder that many mobbing victims like myself go running to HR thinking they are going crazy. Normalcy will always appear crazy when crazy is considered normal.

It was like we were all flying above the ground in our own individual bubbles without actually touching the ground. We were operating in a alternate universe where truth did not exist. Trying to resolve the situation was like grabbing at wind when all these managers and executives had the power to change from one lie to the next to suit the situation. Kristine was the worst of them all. She knew the truth. She could have brought us back to the ground if she had the courage to state that truth. Instead she chose to stay in her bubble of self interest that required her to lie, betray, smear and destroy my reputation and career to save her own.

Late that afternoon, I emailed Kristine telling her that Rick mentioned to me during my second meeting with him that he had spoken to her and that I was surprised about that given the conversation I had with Mike. She replied with: *"He talked with me this afternoon. Do you want to talk tomorrow. Are you okay?"* I don't know how I answered her or if I answered her at all. I think I was feeling okay because I still may have been under the impression that Mike would be meeting with Rick. I can't honestly say that any bells and whistles went off when I read her email, but they sure went off after I created a detailed time line and analysis of the emails two years later for the writing of this book. Both she and Vicky are asking me if I am okay. If I am still there. If I want to talk. Why? She should have been happy about having me come back to HR because it would ease all her concerns about not having enough resources in place while she went out on maternity leave. Instead, she seems very concerned and wants to know if I am okay and want to talk. What did Kristine and Rick discuss in their afternoon meeting to make her wonder if I was all right? I tried to find out the next day when I sent her an email demanding to know what Rick told her but she never answered me.

I worked out in the downstairs gym of the building most days after work and before heading home. This particular evening I cut my workout short because I couldn't stop thinking about Rick once again accusing me of not understanding the change activities. I was getting angrier by the moment and decided to change back into my clothes and go upstairs to see if Mike was still there. He sometimes worked late and there was a good possibility I'd be able to catch him before he left. The door leading into our work area had a glass window. As I looked through it, I saw Rick and Mike sitting at a small conference table outside Mike's office. I assumed Mike was meeting with him on the "team coaching" he talked about with me, so I just turned around and left thinking we would all meet the next day.

When I think about what Rick did next, it absolutely boggles my mind. I understand that I was undeserving of any kind of consideration in his eyes, but to be so inconsiderate of his unscrupulous buddies who were doing everything they could to help him out of the mess he and Stephanie created for themselves defies all logic and comprehension. What his buddies should have realized before laying their integrity and honor on the line for someone like Rick is that narcissistic bullies do not care about anyone but themselves. They will destroy everyone around them if it gets them what they want. Rick wanted to put me down every chance he could. It didn't matter the consequences or who else got hurt. All that mattered was his ego and the satisfaction it got every time he was able to do or say something that annoyed me or made me cry.

The next morning was very quiet. The office almost seemed deserted. Vicky was on vacation, Stephanie and Brandon always traveled back home on Thursday night and Mike was in a conference room on the telephone. Rick and I were the only ones in the work area when I opened a meeting notice from him addressed to Kristine and me with the subject line: "Discuss work plan for Mary." I cannot describe how incensed I was when I saw that subject line. He was making it sound like I was in grade school and my teacher needed to create a special plan for me to follow. Rick's "work plan" terminology was by design. It was not careless wording that we are all guilty of using without thinking. It goes to the core of what he and Stephanie were doing to me from the beginning. It is what all bullies do to their victims and get away with. Words are so powerful. Rick and Stephanie never hit me, they never threatened or yelled at me and until they found themselves in a desperate situation, I can't say they ever lied to me. They were more careful. They had time to slowly chip away at my identity as a talented and creative communications professional.

Rick had been using language as a subtle means of putting me down since I started on the project and the director told him I was the best in my field. I continued to prove my abilities and knowledge and the best he and Stephanie could do was ignore my emails, disparage my work and harass me with subtle put-downs until they were able to chase me away. Rick had been doing this for so long by the time he sent the work plan email that he no longer thought twice about it. This time, he just wasn't so subtle. He was angry that I was still around and he didn't stop to think about how chauvinistic and derogatory his choice of words might sound. He didn't care as long they did the job of putting me in my place. It didn't matter one iota to him that he and Stephanie had included all these other managers and executives in their campaign to get rid of me and his words and actions reflected on them as well.

If it was his goal to get under my skin, then he accomplished it with that meeting notice. As far as I was concerned, that pompous idiot had finally gone over the line and I was shaking with fury as I forwarded the notice to Mike with the following message:

> I met with Rick yesterday and he mentioned again how I didn't understand the change agent strategy. I would like to request a two-minute meeting with you, Rick and Stephanie to state a couple of things for the record and so that we are all on the same page.

It was literally a matter of seconds after sending this email to Mike that Rick was out the door with his back pack in hand. The meeting I requested with Stephanie, Rick and Mike never took place and from that point forward – whether intentionally or not – there was always someone in the work area while I was there with Rick and Stephanie.

Shortly after receiving this meeting notice, I also sent an email to Kristine telling her, "I have no desire to work out a plan with Rick. I would like to know what he told you in his meeting with you." She never answered me. They ignored my requests to get to the bottom of what Rick and Stephanie were saying about me, but naturally the sham meeting to discuss my "work plan" went forward as scheduled. This meeting was nothing but a sloppy attempt to cover up what Kristine and Rick really discussed in their afternoon chat. I have never before been treated the way I was treated in this meeting in any workplace where I have been employed, so my frame of reference is limited. I can only hope that the abuse of power these two people displayed during and after this meeting is a rare occurrence rather than the norm.

This sham meeting began with some chit chat between Rick and Kristine, just like two old friends getting together. We were in the conference room next to Steve's office and at one point, Rick asked if Steve was in the office because his lights were off. I said that Steve always turns his lights out when he leaves his office and Kristine confirmed he was in a meeting with Marcus Fernandez, the CEO of the company. Marcus's office was on the same floor as HR and we all had access to him and knew him well. When I worked for Ed, I sat next to his secretary who sat right outside his office. He said good morning to me every single day. Then, when I transferred to internal communications, Kristine and I were in his office many times to go over various corporate communications. We both worked with him on all the videos he appeared in and I drafted all his messages for the company magazine, along with many of his other communications. I mention my familiarity with Marcus because this was another fact that Vicky tried to gloss over in my final email exchange with her. When I told her my opinion that he was involved in the mobbing, she tried saying he wouldn't recognize either one of us if he ran into us in the hallway. Once again I knew I had hit the right nerve.

But now, back to the meeting. It strikes me as rather strange that Steve wasn't around for this meeting, but it totally confirms my suspicions about their entire strategy to have me terminated before anyone was the wiser. It certainly could have been a coincidence that he was in a meeting with Marcus while Rick and Kristine were playing charades behind his back, but highly unlikely. How was I possibly going to return to HR without Steve's approval? What did they plan on telling him when I moved my things over there? If the intent was to really have me back in HR, then Steve would have had to have known about it – no question. What about all his concerns with headcount? What were they going to do with my replacement? Why didn't he ever talk to me personally about this move? I can only logically conclude that a return to HR was never the intent.

And for that matter, why wasn't Mike invited to this meeting? Yet another member of Rick's team was departing and Rick was down to one member out of the original four. This should have been a concern for Mike. After all, he was the project leader for North America and our team was tasked with the very important assignment of cultivating buy-in among all the employees. After I forwarded the meeting notice to Mike, he never again spoke to me about working with Rick to improve his team coaching skills. He never discussed what he promised at all and it weighed heavily on me. My meeting with him had gone so well and he acted like he understood everything I told him about Rick and Stephanie, yet it appeared he did a complete about-face without talking to me further. It felt like all the forces of the corporation were working against me. I was crying when I finally decided to talk to him and ask him why he changed his mind. He told me it was because he spoke to Rick. He also made an excuse for Rick's work plan terminology and wanted to know if Rick said anything else to me other than what I had already shared with him. I told him Rick had said I didn't want to learn anything. After thinking about it, I remembered it was actually Stephanie who said it, but I didn't bother correcting it. What the hell. It didn't really matter since they would lie about it anyway.

For some reason, there were times when I felt like Mike may have been trying to help me. He came to my desk one time and told me they still wanted me to be their communications person, he made me feel better when I went to him before my last meeting with Kristine and when I told him I would have Kristine review all my work (as Vicky had suggested to me) he told me it would not be necessary. When I mentioned to Vicky that Mike could possibly be trying to help me, she just sloughed off the idea saying, "Do you think any of them care about us? We're just peons in their eyes." I have had to conclude she was honest with me on at least one occasion. Not a single one of them cared about me or my family. They only cared about themselves and their good paying jobs that reimbursed them for incompetence and negligence in their professional duties. Not a one of them has ever contacted me. The company and my colleagues have chosen to act like I never existed and nothing ever happened. Their actions were unconscionable and they have hidden like cowards. Maybe that is just as well because it forced me to eventually face the truth about people like them. It is a truth we must all grapple with if we are to maintain healthy minds and souls in this very unhealthy, egoistic world we inhabit. It took me three years to even consider that Mike and Gary were in on this whole sick charade from the time I wrote the letter to HR. I kept thinking Gary was part of the foreign leadership contingent that Vanessa, Vicky and the others were so afraid of but he was not. He was part of the project leadership contingent; all of whom had their egos and false reputations on the line.

The sham meeting with Rick and Kristine took place on the morning of Wednesday, September 8. For some reason, Mike spoke with Rick and me before this meeting. I honestly do not recall what Mike said to us. I hated Rick so much at that point that I just kind of zoned out and looked at Mike the entire time thinking he was an ally. The only remembrance I have of this encounter is looking at Mike's hands and observing that they were noticeably shaking. He must have been something of a newcomer to the game and was not as well trained in hiding his treachery. That could have been a contributing factor to my stubborn belief that he was somehow trying to help me in the background. He was the worst participant, however, because I now believe he was purposely trying to make me believe he was an ally. I think his hands were shaking because he was exceedingly angry at me. His ego was just as undeservedly big as Rick's and his deceit just as natural. He was the one who told me I would continue to be the communications expert for the project. He was the one who reassured me everything would be fine knowing they were going to terminate my employment. He appeared outwardly as a good family man while inwardly he was nothing but a snake who crawled his way to the top of this hierarchy by compromising every decent quality that defines us as human beings and not as snakes in the grass hiding our true identities so we can bite our enemies before they see us coming. Like Stephanie, Rick, Ed, Marcus, Kristine, Vanessa and all the rest of them, I never saw him coming.

The meeting with Rick and Kristine was humiliation on a grand scale. I might as well have been a plastic, blow-up doll sitting there as they recited their little story line. It went something like this: "So Rick, will Mary continue to do the coordinators' meetings?" "Yes, Kristine. She will continue to take minutes at the meetings." "And Rick, will Mary be attending any of the upcoming meetings on change activities?" "Yes, Kristine. She will attend two or three of them." As the tears welled up in my eyes, I pathetically offered to take over some of Vicky's responsibilities since she was leaving the project and they just looked at one another in silence. I couldn't hold it back any longer and I ran out of the room crying.

I sat outside the building on a bench to gain my composure before going back to my work area. I think I should have stayed outside a little longer. Shortly after returning to my desk, Kristine called me on the telephone. As we were talking, I began sobbing and telling her how I felt like such a failure. Keep in mind that Kristine was aware that everything Rick was saying about me was a lie and she had just actively participated in a meeting, the sole purpose of which was to cover up for Rick's negligence, harassment and lies. As I am crying my heart out not understanding what is happening to me, this contemptible human being tells me I should go see an EAP counselor and says she has done so herself in the past and it has helped her. EAP was the employee assistance program that provided counseling services for various types of problems including mental health, substance abuse and marriage counseling. Mike was sitting at his desk and he didn't come over or say anything to me even though my sobs were audible across the entire floor.

They may have anticipated a crying episode like this occurring after such a malevolent meeting and had their strategy waiting in the wings. Their goal was to make it appear that I was crazy in order to protect themselves in a lawsuit I could have so easily brought against Rick and the company. Stalkers' goals vary from trying to make targets think they are crazy to getting them to become violent so that they can be arrested or forcibly taken to and incarcerated in a psychiatric institution. Some targets are made to suffer so much that they kill themselves or are made so poor that they cannot survive financially. After being forced from their jobs, the gang stalking continues when the company refuses to give the target a good reference. Not being able to find employment (and usually getting blocked from obtaining unemployment payments) the target can quickly find herself broke and homeless after her support system has broken down as a direct result of the gang stalkers' actions. The goal is always to destroy the target emotionally, financially, socially, and physically. Fortunately for me, I had my father, my son and the truth looking out for me.

Kristine knew her referral to the EAP psychologist was totally out of line and malicious but she was weak and willing to do anything they asked her to do. I think it is highly probable they damaged or even destroyed my reputation by following this strategy of mental instability after I walked out on my job the following week. My resignation put them in the position of having to face a potential constructive discharge lawsuit. Constructive discharge is when working conditions become so intolerable as to amount to a firing, despite a lack of a formal termination notice. The fact that I went to my manager over and over again about Rick satisfied the notice requirement that my employer was aware of the conditions and did nothing. Painting me as unbalanced and dangerous would have negated any such claim. I gave them the ammunition they needed when I chose to stare at Stephanie and Rick, stupidly thinking that Mike had my back. I may have inadvertently played into their hands. When I renewed my email correspondence with Vicky, I told her I felt like God had put her on the project for a purpose because if she wasn't there for me, I might have had a nervous breakdown in the lobby of the building. I didn't know then that there is a difference between a nervous breakdown, which is the result of mental illness and a stress breakdown, which is a psychiatric injury brought on by a *normal* reaction to an *abnormal* situation.[9] In her subsequent emails to me, Vicky rarely failed to mention how I was "still healing." I thought she was being a caring friend consoling me over the brutality this spineless group of people inflicted on me. Now that I know Vicky for exactly the person she is and know how desperate they all must have been to cover up what they'd done, I have absolutely no doubt she was trying to establish that I had a nervous breakdown. She didn't know anything about stress injury. They were all worried about getting sued and needed to establish I was unstable if at some point they had to defend themselves in court.

After the sham meeting with Rick and Kristine, my last days on the job were spent in isolation. One of those days was particularly bad and I turned to Vicky for solace. She began by telling me how she had been unfairly treated in the past and she put up with it because she had to. She said it wasn't worth risking my career to file a complaint. She told me they were going to say that Rick said I didn't understand the change activities because I had never worked on the floor in a facility. They were also going to say that they had talked about a work plan. I didn't understand what she meant in saying, "They talked about a work plan," until much later, when I realized that was the cover story they came up with for the meeting Rick had with Kristine in which they discussed the details of my termination the following Monday based on Rick's lies that I was insubordinate when he told me I did not understand the change activities. After finding out that I wrote the change management manual they were going to use going forward, "lack of activities" rather than "not understanding the activities" became the new story line because they could not claim that the author of the change manual for the project did not understand change activities.

That is why Rick had that second meeting with me in the

windowless office. He needed me to actually be insubordinate. When he said that he met with Kristine earlier that day and they decided to send me back to HR due to my lack of understanding, it was a tactical error because he did not know I would send an email to Kristine demanding to know what he said to her. That email was problematic for them. The 'work plan' meeting was meant to resolve that problem by restructuring their strategy. I would continue doing work on the project while there were not many activities going on but I would do it while helping Liz in my old job. This killed two birds with one stone. It alleviated Rick's false allegation of insubordination by replacing it with the lack of activities story line and it put me in a situation where they could let me go because my services were no longer required. Rick's second meeting with me in the windowless office was all Rick's doing. He could not risk having me stick around any longer. It put Stephanie and him in too much danger if I were to leak out anything about the action plan I authored months earlier. He was desperate to make his charge of insubordination stick so I could be fired on the spot.

At the time Vicky told me about their deceitful work plan defense, I was focused on how humiliating and degrading the use of the term was, not the reason for why they had to come up with it in the first place. Vicky knew of this plan of theirs as she was telling me not to file a complaint to save my career. She did such a good job for them in keeping me from going to Vanessa or anyone in HR before they could unfairly terminate me. I know it is a cliche but I really do wonder how she finds it possible to sleep at night. I often try to put myself in all their shoes because it helps me understand their motivations. It is always difficult to do that exercise with Vicky because her actions were so outside the norm for human behavior. She was a voluntary participant. She offered her services to betray me and lie to and about me to destroy my character and professional life. There are no circumstances in my life that I ever would do that to someone.

The meeting with Vicky got very emotional and I got very loud. I said that Rupert Fuller should have done something. Rupert was a director in another area of the organization and Vicky's good friend who she talked to all the time. I think it was Rupert who arranged for Vicky's new job outside the project in an area he supervised. He knew everything going on. She told me Rupert had no obligation to say anything. And then I started yelling, "What about Gary and Mike? They were both mentioned in the letter. Then I asked her, "Why don't you do anything for me?" She got really mad at me when I said that and left the room without saying another word. I ran after her telling her how sorry I was and begging her to forgive me. How sick is she? I mean, really. How sick is that? She appeared to accept my apology, but she refers to this encounter almost a year-and-a-half later in the final email exchange between us as the "first time I accused her of not being my friend." Even sicker. I wish with all my being that I had walked away from her when she left the conference room that day and never looked back. She is the worst person I have ever known.

I didn't do anything those last days except sit at my desk alone reading a book. I was not receiving work, emails or telephone calls from anyone, not even Lynette who had been regularly corresponding with me and giving me work to do. Vicky and I began communicating by paper because I felt very strongly that my emails were being sent to someone to review so that Kristine and the others could be told how to respond to me. This became particularly evident my final weekend there, which I talk about a bit later. If it was legal cover they wanted, Ed was the only one who could have been tasked with that duty. The attorney and ethics officer who should have come to my rescue was instead one of the corporate gang members who stalked me. I was essentially trapped. There was absolutely no one to turn to and that is why they felt so confident in bouncing me around, changing stories and lying about me without blinking an eye. Talk about an evil place. This was it. The best argument in keeping your workplace ethical is shown by the incompetence and cronyism that defined this place. They couldn't even accomplish the simple job of getting me fired.

Power abusers like Rick have no problem with lying and are very good at convincing others that the victim is the one at fault. As people turn on the target and the campaign against her gains strength, the target begins to stress out and eventually makes a mistake. It is a common occurrence in mobbing situations for the person being ganged up on to lash out emotionally and do something inappropriate. The bully will then use this outburst to turn the tables on the target and convince everyone that she is the instigator of the trouble. Management then has an excuse to take disciplinary action against the target, up to and including termination.

This is exactly what happened to me. While shy, I am not compliant. I usually do not back down when I know I am right. I may get emotional and shake and shiver while stating my position, but I will not fail to take every opportunity to do so. This can be an excellent quality if you are able to remain in control of your emotions and think about your arguments rationally. I was doing neither the day Mike met with us to go over the survey results. The meeting room was in the other building, so Vicky and I walked over together. At the time, I felt like we were comrades in arms in this battle together. I thought Rick and Stephanie had treated her as shabbily as me when they made her go on the trip overseas and then would not allow her to attend any of the meetings. I was feeling defiant and even said to her, "You're really in the cat bird's seat," making a reference to the fact she was black and a woman. She just smiled at me coyly and said she never heard that expression before. Yeah, right.

I sat in the front of the room for the meeting, Vicky sat directly behind me and Rick and Stephanie sat together in the back row. Shortly after Mike started the meeting, I turned my chair around and just began staring at Rick and Stephanie. It was a pretty threatening and an absolutely stupid thing to do, particularly since other people were there to witness it. However, in my eyes, the object card plays both ways. Rick and Stephanie felt no guilt or shame in lying and ruining my reputation, so I felt no obligation in treating them with anything resembling respect. Although I still feel the same way, this was such a miscalculation on my part. It actually gave them a viable reason to fire me for insubordination. It also gave them credibility if they tried to portray me as being emotionally unstable after I walked out. No one but their accomplices and them would ever have to know the back story.

The bad team survey results were never discussed in this meeting meant for discussing the results. In a heated email exchange to Vicky a little more than a year later, I speculated that the reason the results weren't discussed was because they couldn't risk having the action plan I sent to Rick more than three months earlier come up in the discussion. I have no doubt that the bad results and feedback on the survey matched the feedback I received from all the team members.

Cowards always look for the easy way out and I gave it to them by staring at Stephanie and Rick. All the brutality they heaped on me was amusing, but as soon as the tables got turned and I gave them just a tad of their own medicine, they went whining like little babies to Mike demanding that something be done with me. I don't know what Mike told them because I didn't talk to any of them about it and they didn't talk to me. However, since confronting the truth that Mike was in on the whole thing, I figure he probably just told them to wait it out one more day. I would be gone on Monday and they couldn't risk any confrontations before then that would force them to regroup and again alter their strategy.

Kristine's final meeting with me was late on the Friday afternoon before my planned termination on the following Monday. This meeting was precipitated by a quick succession of emails that were exchanged between the two of us earlier in the afternoon. In the first email to her, I apologized for staring at Rick and Stephanie and told her that I just wanted some resolution to everything that was happening so that I could concentrate on my work and life again. At the time, I was neither eating nor sleeping and was frantic over what was happening around me although I had no idea what was actually happening to me. I was in a heightened state of stress and anxiety that was leaving me feeling hopeless and helpless as they were knowingly and consciously plotting my demise and enjoying all the side-benefits of watching me lose my mind trying to fight the unknown enemies plotting against me in secret behind closed doors.

I suggested to Kristine that she could handle the communications for me if she felt the situation was beyond repair. She emailed back to me saying I could come talk to her, but she thought she had made things clear in the [sham] meeting with Rick and me. After having her tell me that, I knew it was pointless talking to her. I decided instead to talk to Mike. I told him that I would have Kristine look over all my work, as Vicky had suggested, but he said that wouldn't be necessary. I also said how sorry I was for staring at Rick and he told me not worry about it – that time heals all wounds. He told me this knowing I was getting fired. This was a totally amoral and cruel man. Yet, just like the company attorney and ethics officer, he comes off as the consummate family man. How could such good fathers be so cruel? That is what all the bystanders and enablers think and so naturally they blame the victims and justify in their minds that they deserve to be the brunt of this unbridled cruelty.

I didn't want to stay in the work area with Rick and Stephanie any longer, so I decided to move my folders and office supplies over to HR. I packed up a cart and wheeled it over to the other building before my meeting with Kristine. The cubicle she assigned to me to was covered with boxes and all the drawers were locked with no keys to open them. She obviously never planned on having me move into it. Not being able to move any of my belongings into the locked up desk that Kristine sent me to, I left the unpacked cart in the cubicle and went to talk to her. A man was standing in the doorway of her cubicle talking to her when I approached, so I went to Vanessa's cubicle instead. She sat in the next cubicle over. Vanessa was talking to one of the HR generalists she worked with and without even thinking, I walked right in on them and with tears in my eyes I said to Vanessa, "I think I am going crazy." She just responded with a reassuring smile saying, "You're not going crazy." The generalist looked uncomfortable and left. Vanessa was uncomfortable too and told me I should really be talking to Kristine. I know now that the reason she tried to push me off on Kristine was because they couldn't have HR knowing anything until I was gone if their plausible deniability strategy was to work. When she peered over the cubicle wall, she saw that Kristine was still talking to the man. She told me she didn't know him and didn't feel comfortable talking around him, so she took me to a cubicle in the next row.

Everything was beginning to feel strange to me then so I didn't think it peculiar that she didn't want a man she didn't know to hear what we were saying. Whenever I think about it now, the whole HR area appears dark and gloomy in my mind. I think it's because that afternoon marked the end of my life as I had always known it. It was the start of my mind's entrance into the very scary realm of disassociation from reality. This is a common symptom of PTSD. From there on out, I would find myself having to navigate on intuition alone – not knowing where I was, where I was going or where I would end up. It is no wonder if I sounded crazy when I started asking Vanessa questions like, "Hypothetically, if someone says things to you that aren't true, what should you do?" and "Hypothetically, if a supervisor tells you you don't understand something and you do, what should you do?" That is not ordinarily how I speak to people. I always try to be forthright and upfront. I would never have nervously skirted around this issue with vague hypothetical statements if I had been in a normal state of mind. I was simply scared and did not know who to trust.

Vanessa told me that there was nothing HR could do if I didn't file a complaint. I didn't want to file a complaint. I never wanted to file a complaint. I just wanted someone to help me. I sincerely thought Vanessa could be that person because I liked and trusted her. Knowing now how deeply she was involved and how she would have been the likely one to fire me the next Monday, telling me to file a complaint was really the best she could offer. How's that for an effective HR manager and department? Tell an employee to file a complaint against the company you are hired to protect. Oh, I forgot. She had nothing to worry about because they already had their defenses lined up as Vicky so graciously let me know.

By now, Kristine had finished her conversation and as we began walking down the hallway on the way to the conference room for our meeting, I saw that Steve was in a closed door meeting with Roberta. In my mind's eye, that meeting looked staged. That would make sense because they couldn't risk having this whole thing blow up in their faces by having me go to Steve or filing a complaint before I got terminated on Monday. However, just because they didn't want me going to Steve doesn't mean he didn't know about everything. It simply provided them with the cover they'd need in the event I filed a lawsuit *after* they fired me. They could all say they didn't know anything about Rick's harassment because I never went to anyone about it.

Kristine and I continued past Steve's office and into the conference room where I had my very last encounter with Kristine. It was contentious from the moment we sat down. Kristine displayed a side of herself I had never seen before. I was expecting it to be like any of the other conversations we had with one another, but there were to be no pleasantries here. She immediately started in asking me about how I was going to be able to work with Rick. I asked her to call Vanessa in and we could all talk about it. She wouldn't do that. She just kept asking how I was going to be able to work with Rick. When I repeated that we should have Vanessa come in to talk about it, she refused. We were both getting heated up at one another, going back and forth. But then I began to panic and my mouth became very dry, so I asked her if I could go get a drink of water. My hands were shaking when I returned to the meeting room, but when I sat down and told her that Mike said time heals all wounds, her whole demeanor changed. She quit questioning me and began telling me how I could help my replacement with some of the writing for the Intranet because she was having a hard time keeping up with it.

All her questions about working with Rick were no doubt her own attempt at getting me to be insubordinate. With insubordination, they could cleanly terminate my employment and not have to deal with the mess of any potential lawsuit. I have no doubt she emailed her handlers while I was getting water and they told her to quit trying to make me angry for purposes of insubordination since Mike had said that time heals all wounds. They could not have a war of directors with one telling me that the staring incident was not a problem since time heals all wounds and the other brow beating me over how I was going to work with him.

Too bad I didn't realize much sooner that Kristine and I were working off different playbooks. If she had any respect for me, she would have found a way to spare me the degrading send-off she gave me. She knew I was getting fired the following Monday. She could have ended this meeting after she was told to cancel her attempt at insubordination. Or she could have told me we would go over my plan after I had a chance to get settled back in on Monday – even if it would have been a lie. She certainly had no trouble with lying. No.

This meeting was her only opportunity to drive the last nail into this whistle blower's coffin and make sure that if I had a shred of confidence left in me when I entered the conference room, I wouldn't when I left. As Kristine did with all her work – she made sure she did a perfect job. I left there with nothing after being told how I could help Liz out with work she couldn't keep up with – the same work I always kept up with by staying late night after night and working weekends to complete.

Divine Intervention

That night, I went to dinner and a play with a friend of mine. I am surprised he ever called me again after my appalling behavior that evening. I couldn't stop thinking about everything. I was sending email messages under the table and making the conversation all about HR. It was so rude and unlike me. At the play, I couldn't focus on what was happening. I couldn't make decent conversation. My heart was racing. I was fixated on that last meeting with Kristine. In the car ride home, I sent her an email asking her why she sent me to a desk with boxes and locked drawers. She didn't respond to it, just as she didn't respond to any of the emails I sent her that weekend. At least not the way any person with feelings and empathy would. As I became increasingly desperate, so did the emails I was sending out. They all expressed my desperation and anger. No one was responding to any of them until they were told when and how to answer them and the responses that came back to me were just as cold as all their hearts.

The next two days were the worst two days of my life. I say that unequivocally and without question. Insanity must feel a lot like the way I felt. That is why it is so strange that somehow the most clarity I have ever displayed in my life came through in the midst of such mental chaos. My final emails could almost create an outline for what Rick, Stephanie, Kristine, Vanessa, Ed, Vicky, Roberta and the others were planning behind the scenes for me when I arrived to work on Monday.

"Headcount. It sure is a good thing I know how to write a good letter." That was the text of the first email I sent to Vanessa that weekend. I had no idea what it meant. I just knew that headcount was a bad thing because Vicky put it into my head when she said that Steve and Rick discussed it in their meeting after I wrote the letter to HR. Headcount turned out to be the basis of their strategy to fire me before I went back to HR with any damaging information or complaint that would bring to light Rick's incompetence, Rick's harassment of me and Rick and Stephanie's intentional attempts to cover up and hide their professional negligence and harassment.

They thought they would have more time to pay off Nicole and Vicky for their silence, get some more damaging information on me and then torture or bore me to death so that I would eventually quit, or slip up and give them an excuse to fire me. They were able to get the jobs for Vicky and Nicole. They were also very close to getting me to quit when I wrote the email to Kristine saying how useless I felt and wanted off the project. She replied with, "Ha, ha, ha, ha" not because she was happy, but rather out of a sense of relief at being able to follow through on what I think their original plan was. Once they got me back to HR working as a floater, they could tell me my services were no longer required and let me go. In my last round of emails to Vicky (when I still thought she was a friend) she fell back on this original strategy in her robotic defense of their actions. When I told her my theory that they were going to fire me the following Monday for staring at Rick and Stephanie, she pooh poohed it and said that wasn't a reason for firing me. Her denial told me I was right. She then qualified her denial by saying it didn't mean they weren't going to fire me at some point later on.

That is another reason I have found for being thankful. If I had returned to HR, they would have made my life a living hell and I would have suffered psychological damage from which I never would have recovered. I try not to focus on all the scheming, lying and planning that was done behind my back. I try always to focus on and thank God every day for my wonderful life. I am healthy in mind, body and soul and am one of the very fortunate ones who realize that is all that matters in this illusory world we have created for ourselves. There is a limit to what people can endure. As far as I am concerned, I was subjected to nothing less than mental torture my final weeks on the job. If I would have had to go home to my son and father and tell them I was fired, I would not have survived it. There is no way I would have been able to process such an injustice in the mental state I was in. Unlike the workplace and school shooters who have shot people after having been bullied and mobbed, I would have killed myself. I saved myself from that fate by emailing Kristine asking her what she and Rick discussed in their meeting. I thank God that Rick was so desperate and stupid. If he hadn't told me about his meeting with Kristine, prompting me to send her the email, I would not be here typing these words. I would have walked into their trap and been taken completely by surprise when Vanessa met with me to tell me I was being laid off due to lack of activities. My email to Kristine demanding to know what Rick said to her in their meeting forced them to regroup. They came up with the work plan story because it would not have worked to their advantage to have it become known that Rick and Kristine discussed my unlawful termination in their meeting. They had to keep me on for another week to cover their bases and that additional week saved my life. Their actions became so outlandish and absurd from then on that the only logical choice they left me with was to leave on my own.

4

THE WEEKEND FROM HELL

My Telephone Call With Ed

On Saturday morning, I tried calling Vicky but her phone went straight to voice mail. I left a message, but she never called back. There was no one to talk to and my mind was going wild. You cannot imagine the sense of frustration and stress that builds in a person when no one is communicating with them or when they do communicate, it is with lies or purposely calculated, machine-like replies. This had been going on for the past two weeks and I couldn't take it anymore. I just began pacing back and forth down the hallway to my bedroom, then to the living room, then to the kitchen and back again. I wanted to scream, cry out, yell ... something to find some relief.

Even if their heartlessness and contempt prevented them from treating me in a humane way, there were two emails I sent that day that should have set the alarm bells off for any HR manager or attorney who is worth a fraction of their pay. In the first of these two emails, I wrote to Vanessa, "Don't they watch the news. The cover-up is always worse than the crime." I really don't know why I wrote it. It could have been because what they did to me felt criminal, or should be criminal. The second email was also sent to Vanessa telling her I would sign any legal papers they wanted me to sign absolving the company of any liability. Mind you, she is the one who spoke with me and told me to write the letter to the HR vice president. She is the one I went to the day earlier and asked what someone should do in a "hypothetical" case of harassment and she is the one who responded by saying HR cannot do anything unless that person files a complaint. Of course hindsight is always 20-20, but as I see it now (with a clear head and focus), she is at a critical juncture here. She has several options. She could call me, but that probably wouldn't be advisable until she first spoke with Steve or the company's general counsel to get their advice as to what she should say. She could ignore it and run the risk of having the company deal with a constructive discharge lawsuit if I quit. She could have me come in and sign the papers knowing that they all knew Rick had acted negligently and were already building their defenses in the event I took her up on her advice to file a complaint. She could lie and tell me she would be available later in the week to talk knowing that she was going to fire me on Monday. She chose the last option.

I didn't consciously know when I sent the emails to Vanessa that I was going to be fired, but I did know I couldn't go back to HR. Not like this - with everyone thinking I had failed at this assignment. I decided to turn in my resignation instead. I sent an email to Kristine telling her I was resigning and another one to Vanessa telling her I would leave my phone and badge in the downstairs lobby. Of course, neither one of them responded to me. They must have been told not to by the man - or men - behind the scenes pulling their strings. I still wonder how that was done. They wouldn't have wanted to leave any kind of paper trail. I don't know if they were calling each other on their private cell phones or if they all met at the office that weekend knowing I would be gone by Monday. It would be extremely ironic if they were all at the office as you will soon see.

Having come this far, I decided to play the last card in my deck and I called my old boss whose job it was to handle ethics complaints. I had very little contact with Ed after I transferred to communications. I wouldn't describe the relationship as bad. It was more like neither one of us really liked each other or felt comfortable around one another after I quit working for him. I would never have called him if I had not felt so desperate for someone to respond to me and do something. He was literally my very last chance for getting any kind of justice.

There was a problem in contacting him though. I didn't have his telephone number in my blackberry. Frank, the director of public relations I mentioned earlier, must have emailed me called me recently because I had his number handy. I knew he worked closely with Ed and would have his number, but I also trusted and respected Frank and felt very comfortable turning to him. When I called him my mind was reeling. I was extremely stressed and nervous. When I asked to meet with Ed and him at the office he was very willing to do so and even asked me if I needed him to drive me there because I sounded very distraught. When I told him I'd be fine, he gave me Ed's number and told me to call him back after I spoke with him.

Knowing the extent of Ed's involvement as I think I do now, I am a little surprised he answered his phone when I called him. It would have made more sense to have it go into voice mail like Vicky's did, unless of course he didn't want a record of the call. For whatever reason, he answered. I identified myself and told him I needed to talk to him about something illegal that was going on. Like the email I sent to Vanessa where I referred to a cover up and crime, I don't know why I used the word "illegal" with Ed. I certainly wasn't looking at the experience in those terms at all at the time. At least, not consciously. Unjust, yes. Unethical, yes. Immoral, yes. But not criminal. I had not at that time tied Rick and Stephanie's harassing behavior to their attempt to cover-up their negligence by getting me fired. Even if this behavior is not criminal, it should be. No one should have to withstand the kind of emotional and psychological assault I was subjected to in order to hide another person's negligence. The parent company overseas was either aware of it as it was happening or became aware of it later when I contacted them, but it didn't matter. They got what they wanted when I didn't sue and I have never heard from any of them ever again.

Ed quickly picked up on my use of the term and I backed up by assuring him I didn't mean to say illegal. He told me he really shouldn't be talking to me but to go ahead and tell him what I had to say. I was sounding just as frantic as I did when I spoke with Frank and my voice was shaking as I told him that I really needed to meet with him in person at the office to talk. For as long as I live, I will never forget the irritation I heard in his voice as he told me in an exasperated tone, "I'm with my kids." He made me feel like such a nuisance for calling him on the weekend.

Just like Vanessa though, he hadn't allowed himself many options other than to shirk his responsibilities as the chief ethics officer and attorney for the company. Ed was already knee deep in this cover up. I come to that conclusion because of his statement that he shouldn't be talking to me and because of his subsequent treatment of me. But what if he hadn't been involved in it? What if my phone call was the first he heard anything about it? Here he has a distraught, former employee of his calling him and telling him something illegal is going on. In this situation, what are his obligations as the general counsel and chief ethics officer of the corporation? When I told my friend about it, he said Ed could not meet with me because of any potential legal liability he did not yet know about and from which he would need to protect the company. Of course, this wasn't the case with Ed but it got me thinking. Should an attorney also hold the title of ethics officer? Is there an inherent conflict of interest there? I wasn't going to Ed as an attorney for the company. I was going to him in his capacity as the company's chief ethics officer. All Ed knew from my initial statement was that something illegal may be going on. In his capacity as the company's ethics officer, I think his first obligation should have been to get at the root of what I was calling about and make certain that I truly was incorrect in using that terminology to describe the situation.

I was extremely upset when I called Ed. Even though he would try to have me believe otherwise at the conclusion of our call, I did gradually calm down as I relayed my story. I don't recall telling him much, if anything, about Rick and Stephanie's bullying. Instead, I focused on the more recent events of the mobbing. I remember specifically telling him about Rick's false assertion that I didn't understand the change activities and having Rick tell me he would speak to Mike when I said I wanted talk to Steve about getting off the project. I also told him about Kristine's comment that I was dealing with power and that I should apologize to Rick.

After I finished telling him about Rick's harassment, Kristine's comment about power and the fact that Rick did not want me going to the HR vice president, can you guess what he said to me? He told me I sounded like I was close to a breakdown and asked me if I had anyone to talk to. I know I promised no commentary but I think this statement of his following on the heels of what I had just told him requires at least a little analysis.

Unfortunately, I had the displeasure of working for this man. He was the last person I wanted to call. Neither one of us wanted to be having this telephone conversation. I wasn't expecting warm and fuzzy from Ed. What I was expecting was for him to do his job. If I take my statement about illegal activity out of it - and even if I take all the emails I was sending out of it - one of things I specifically recall telling him is that Kristine told me that I was "dealing with power." When you combine that statement with the other details I provided to him, it creates an undeniable case of unethical behavior. He should have packed his kids in the car at that point (actually they were old enough to take care of themselves) and taken the five minute drive from his house to the office to meet with me. He didn't do that. He didn't even ask me to elaborate on it over the telephone or to meet with him on Monday. Instead he told me that I sounded like I was close to a breakdown. You can call me emotional. You can call me overly dramatic. You can even call me crazy if you like, but there have been whistle blowers who crossed paths with power and ended up dead. It was this man's job to protect the integrity of the company and the safety of its employees. My friend is wrong when he says that Ed could not meet me because of legal considerations. He had an absolute obligation to meet with me and anyone else he had to in order to get to the bottom of this story I just related to him. But then again, he knew the story better than anyone else and getting to the bottom of it was not a part of the story line.

He seemed a little nervous when I told him I had written an email to Kristine and Vanessa handing in my resignation, and together we decided that I should write to Kristine and tell her I wasn't resigning. He also said he would talk to her on Monday and when I asked if he wanted me to join them, he said "no." I had vacation time left and when I suggested taking it the next week, Ed agreed. I was also bothered by the cover-up email I sent to Vanessa earlier in the day and I mentioned it to him before concluding our conversation. He was so reassuring when he told me, "Oh, I don't think that's a problem." He closed by telling me he would call Frank back for me. I assume he did because I never heard from Frank again.

I thought Ed would talk to Kristine and an investigation would ensue. Having worked as a paralegal for civil defense firms for almost seven years before working in corporate law, I have a good idea of how the law works. I knew, without question, that I would not be suing the company. I wanted to do something that would limit their liability and allow them to conduct an investigation without fear of a looming lawsuit. It probably wasn't the brightest thing I have ever done in my life because Vicky later told me it gave Vanessa a good excuse for not investigating further. That was my intent, however, when I sent an email to Mike asking him to relay my apologies to Rick and Stephanie and tell them I might have misunderstood them when they said I didn't understand the change activities. I also sent an email to Lynette telling her that my husband and I were thinking of moving to Georgia. I figured if they thought I was moving out-of-state, then they would definitely conclude I wasn't planning a lawsuit.

These were impulsive and ill-thought out moves for sure, but I was winging it at this point. Everything I was doing that weekend was intuitive and emotional, rather than rational and thoughtful. I don't regret any of my actions because I was incapable of acting any other way. These people had driven me to a state of frenzy, darkness and despair that no person should ever be taken to by people they work with and trust.

Below is a list of emails I remember sending out that Friday night and Saturday afternoon. There were even more. I didn't save all of them. As you read them, you will see a person in complete desperation and panic. None of these people had the decency, courage or compassion to step forward and admit they had gone over the line - that what they did was wrong. They put this company in unbelievable jeopardy in every possible way. And they put themselves and other employees in physical danger. A human being has just so much mental endurance. I was at the end of mine.

Day	Email Text
Fri	**To Vanessa:** I understand now. Thanks for listening. It just takes some time to deal with total and complete disillusionment. I will report to work Monday with a smile on my face and acting like nothing ever happened.

	No response
Fri	**To Kristine:** Asking her why she sent me to desk with boxes and locked drawers No response
Sat	**To Kristine:** I was doing some homework today for a class I am taking. For some reason I thought of something you told me awhile back in one of our meetings. You said I wasn't the kind of manager the company looks for and you encouraged me to pursue a different career path. You were right. Thanks for your guidance. No response
Sat	**To Vanessa:** Headcount. It sure is a good thing I know how to write a good letter. No response
Sat	**To Vanessa:** I just can't get anyone to answer my emails anymore. They should watch the news more often and they would learn the cover up is always worse than the crime. No response
Sat	**To Kristine:** How could you? No response
Sat	**To Mike and Lynette**

	Telling them not to use any of the materials I prepared. Wrote them back a little later telling them they could use them.
	No response from Mike. Got a response later from Lynette telling me that Rick and Stephanie can be difficult people to work with but …
Sat	**To Kristine:**
	Handing in my resignation.
	No response
Sat	**To Vanessa:**
	Saying I was resigning and would leave name tag and blackberry downstairs in lobby.
	No response
Sat	**To Vanessa:**
	Telling her I would never use my words again to give credit to any organization or individual who did not deserve it.
	No response
Sat	**To Vanessa:**
	Telling her I would sign legal papers absolving company of any liability. Just wanted to move on positively.
	She writes back saying she is unaware of any problems and would be available sometime the next week to talk.
Sat	**Called Ed:**
	Telling him what was happening to me.

> He tells me it sounds like I am close to a breakdown and asks if I
> have anyone to talk to. I tell him no – my husband and I have
> separated. As if of no interest, he tells me the emails I sent about a
> cover-up and headcount are no problem.

Many victims of bullying and mobbing will kill themselves before they kill someone else. However, there are many instances of workplace and school shootings where a victim has become violent and killed people. I am not a violent person and I am so glad I don't own a gun because they drove me to state of temporary insanity that weekend. The person who was sending out one email after another was not me. It was a broken and lost person who was desperately reaching out to have someone acknowledge her. I had become a complete stranger to myself and remained so for a very long time afterward.

On the following Monday after calling Ed, I was standing in my kitchen when I did receive an email. It was the only email that I received in a couple of weeks that wasn't initiated by me. It was from my old teammate, Nicole. I hadn't spoken or communicated with her since they paid her off with a new job on a different team. She was the last person I expected to hear from, but she was the only one they could use to send me a message they very much wanted me to have after calling Ed. When I opened it and read "Traitor" with a smiley face beside it, I was so frightened I immediately deleted it after reading her short message welcoming me back to HR.

I couldn't wait any longer to hear back from him so I called Ed myself on Wednesday to see if he had met with Kristine. That same morning, I sent an email to Vanessa asking for a leave of absence in order to to buy some time. The excuse I used was that my husband and I were separated and my father was in ill health. Instead of answering my question about whether or not he had spoken to Kristine, Ed told me he didn't want to pry but was curious about what the psychiatrist told me. This inquiry is downright creepy. I even thought it was weird when he asked it. I called Ed thinking by this time he would be conducting an in-depth investigation and getting further details from me and everyone else about what I told him on Saturday. Instead he is sounding like some old gossip fishing for information with his question about what I told the psychiatrist I never went to see.

After saying something like I didn't want to talk about it, Ed did what he always did with ethical concerns that came to him. He sent me to the handlers in HR saying, "I can't really help you. You need to talk to someone in HR about this." I must have had my doubts about Steve Argon even then because when Ed told me I needed to talk to someone in HR, I answered, "Even Steve?" When he said, "Yes," I hung up the phone, got my purse, got in my car and drove straight to the office to quit. I didn't even wait to hear back from Vanessa after realizing it was futile to try to buy time with a leave of absence. There was no way out for me and although I did not know the details of their efforts to banish me, I knew all roads to any kind of resolution were closed tight. It might actually have been beneficial to them if I had taken Ed up on his suggestion to go to HR because they already had their defenses lined up. Maybe that was his intention. I don't know because that was the last time I ever spoke to Ed. I never told him about my intention not to sue and I am pretty sure I never told Vicky either. Hopefully, they all had some sleepless nights worrying about it at least a little.

By the time it got to the point of calling Ed and not getting any resolution, I can't really think of anything I could have done except what I did. As I entered the building, I thought they may have deactivated my badge and it wouldn't work in the elevator, but it did. I went straight to Kristine's cubicle. She looked all small and hunched over as I *placed* my badge and blackberry on the desk in front of her. I put the word "placed" in italics because Vicky told me she heard that I threw my phone at Kristine. She was very surprised to see me and looked absolutely pitiful when she whispered, "I wish Vanessa was here." How sad for her. She was just so ill equipped to deal with it all. As I turned to leave, she got up and said, "Mary, let's talk – not like leader to employee, but one-on-one." When I said to her, "Okay, but no games," she just stood there and said nothing. I continued out and she ran after me asking me what the psychiatrist told me.

It was like swimming upstream. I had the forces of management working against me, but I also had my own negative emotions and stress to contend with. If I had been able to control the amount of stress I was feeling, I may have been better able to retain a level of clarity that allowed me to seek out more constructive solutions. Instead, I let myself get too emotional. This has been a bad habit of mine since as far back as I can remember and it is still the one area in which I have the most difficulty changing. In all honesty though, there were very few, if any, solutions to be had. The goal with mobbing is to eliminate solutions in an effort to get rid of the target. In my case, I have concluded there was nothing I could have done to help myself. My letter to HR implicated *all* the power players in this saga. Unfortunately none of them had the character or awareness to confront the issues or their shortcomings until I was gone.

In our various email exchanges after I left the company, Vicky told me that Lynette and her team leader were off the project, the consulting company was fired and Rick was reassigned. Lynette and her team leader were doomed because neither of them worked in a facility either, which was the excuse they came up with for Rick accusing me of not understanding the change activities. Like Vicky and Nicole, I am sure they were properly compensated for their transfers. I do not know how they shaped the story to justify the firing of the consulting company and the reassignment of Rick but I do know my role was not mentioned. My legacy is as the crazy employee who had a nervous breakdown and ran out throwing her phone at Kristine. This is what corrupt people do. They manipulate events in order to shape history in their favor and justify their actions. I placed my phone on Kristine's desk when I went in to quit after all roads to a solution had been closed off. She is the crazy one who went chasing after me as I walked away asking me what I told the psychiatrist she suggested I go see. I turned around and told her he said that they should all feel icky. Although I never went to see a psychiatrist, I feel fairly confident in speaking for the psychiatric community when I described their actions as icky. This corrupt group of executives and managers obviously set themselves up as the saviors of the situation once I was gone. They took my letter, my ideas and my work and claimed them as their own. Jesus said there is a special place in hell for people like them and I cannot help but agree with him.

How could so many people make decisions that were so antithetical to the values they were supposed to uphold? What would motivate them to act so contrary to everything they had been taught in their human resources, legal and leadership training? What would make a director of communications, whose job it was to convey the importance of transparency and face-to-face communication to everyone else, feel like she could lie to my face and then refer me to a psychiatrist when I became upset over it? What would make an attorney acting as the chief ethics officer of the company act so unethically himself and put the company he was hired to protect in severe legal and physical jeopardy? What would make an HR manager ignore an employee who is describing a situation of harassment to her and then act so cavalier when that same employee offers to sign legal papers absolving the company of liability? What would make a bullying manager feel like he can act with impunity and continue to subject that same employee to harassment after it has been brought to his attention by a superior? What makes a colleague kick you when you are down and accuse you of being a traitor for reporting misconduct? What makes a director fabricate a story to cover up another person's tracks? What makes a person pretend to be a friend and continue that pretense long after it serves its purpose?

The people who bullied and mobbed me included eight executives at the manager level and above, four of whom worked in HR, one of whom was the general counsel and chief ethics officer of the corporation, and all of whom purposefully and maliciously set out to destroy the professional and personal life of an employee in their care. There are no acceptable reasons for this behavior. NONE.

When I called Ed, all I knew was that I was being unfairly treated and no one wanted to do anything about it. I didn't know about Rick and Stephanie's fear of being exposed for negligence. You cannot harass, purposely try to get someone fired, plan defenses in advance, threaten them with an email calling them traitorous, level false accusations of mental instability against them, tell lies about them, gang stalk them by sending people into where they go to harass them and make them paranoid – all to get around the law. I did what the company asked its employees to do and was punished beyond all comprehension for it. It is totally irrational and cruel. This company and other companies like it who tell their employees one thing and then punish them for doing it will pay a horrible price. If I have learned anything at all through this experience, it is that if an organization truly believes its values are worthy of being followed then they better walk the walk. If they are incapable or unwilling to do so, then they will have a cynical, fearful, and resigned workforce unable to be innovative and creative because of the consequences they perceive will befall them. They will be paranoid and on the lookout for spies in all departments. They will let power intimidate them into doing things that are unimaginable in a normal and honest environment. They will view themselves and colleagues as peons without a voice. They will betray and lie to their co-workers to advance their own agendas. They will steal from the coffers. They will do all these things and more because they are just following the deceitful example the organization set for itself by lying to them with a set of values that were never followed by those at the top. Better not to have any values at all than to create this kind of hell existing in unreality.

When I called Ed, all I knew was that I was being unfairly treated and no one wanted to do anything about it. I didn't know about Rick and Stephanie's fear of being exposed for negligence. Maybe Ed didn't know about it either, but he did know that Rick was harassing me. He also knew they were planning on firing me or he wouldn't have been so nervous about my resignation and anxious about getting me to withdraw it. He didn't want to face a constructive discharge lawsuit and if he was worth the several hundred thousand dollars he was getting paid, he would have had me sign the legal papers I offered to sign.

We live in a world of cell phones, twitter, Facebook, the web, instant messaging and email; yet we don't know how to talk to each other. Other than Mike, whose only reason for talking to me was to give me false assurances until they could fire me a few days later, none of these managers ever bothered to get my side of the story. I wasn't worth it. Do you know what that does to a person when you reduce them to the status of an object to be kicked around at will? I'll tell you. They get angry, confused, frustrated and revengeful. There are no words to express the contempt I felt toward Ed and the others. They need to know that what they did wasn't fun. It isn't what is done in business and they were not just doing their jobs. There are often dire consequences when you play with people in this manner and bend the rules to suit your own desires.

There was a court case against a major corporation where a store employee who had been verbally bullied for two years was fired. She had made management aware of the bullying behavior and nothing was done. After she was terminated, she went back to the store and shot and killed the man who was harassing her. She also went into the store and shot at other store employees as well. The events leading up to the shooting are eerily similar to what happened to me and the store is now being sued for negligence in the way it handled the termination by the estate of the man who was shot.

By the time I called Ed, I was begging for help. If I had not called him and showed up for work the following Monday, they would have terminated my employment as planned. The company that so callously treated me like a rag doll to be manipulated and thrown around at will should thank God every day that I did not own a gun at the time they stole my life and mind. It would have been so easy in my haste to go resign to slip it in my purse. My ego was in charge then. I honestly do not know what I would have done. Ed, Kristine, Vanessa, Rick and the other managers and executives didn't know what I would have done either. Since Ed so dismissively told me I sounded like I was close to a breakdown with no further follow-up or concern, I can only assume they never had any intention of letting me into the building when I showed up on Monday. If I had gone on a shooting rampage like the store employee, the postal workers or like so many other students who have been bullied, they would have called me insane (which they were already doing) and put the blame for any fatalities solely on my shoulders. They would have used my phone call to Ed and Frank as evidence of instability and my manager and co-workers would have backed them up with great relief and with absolutely no guilt over their culpability. My family would have had to live with the shame of having their mother, wife and daughter labeled a vicious killer and there would have been no one to tell the real story of how this gang intentionally perpetrated a psychological assault on an innocent victim because she had the nerve to state the truth about the incompetence of one of their buddies in management. The newspapers would have repeated their lies without delving any further into why a motivated and passionate employee who excelled at her job four months earlier and had recently enrolled in a master's program suddenly became a mass murderer.

My original thesis was that not a one of them had the courage to speak up. That's not it at all. They wouldn't have known the right thing to do if it hit them in the face because they were all accustomed to doing the wrong thing. It wasn't just Rick who was afraid of exposure. Once the survey results came back reflecting many of the concerns I raised in the letter and the action plan, they all became fearful because they ignored the letter. They simply relied on the same strategies they always relied on when one of their own in management was caught with his hand in the cookie jar or his ineptitude caused a problem. They used the good 'ol boy network and its allies in HR to cover up the crime and get rid of anyone who was highlighting the crime. Unfortunately for me, the fear spread from one manager to the next until it reached the man at the top of the hierarchy who would have been shown the letter and chose to protect them. Along with Ed, he used the power of his office to orchestrate the mobbing. It is why everyone was able to lie and manipulate circumstances at will. The man at the top allayed all their fears when he told them they would be protected if they would just do as he and Ed said. There is no force more powerful than fear and no greater comfort than having someone with the power to do it say you have nothing to fear. I will take care of it. And took care of it he did. I was trapped because the ultimate authority decided to trap me and let his managers enjoy the fruits of their labor in destroying me for questioning them.

5

Strategies For Confronting Abuse Of Power

The First Step In Combating Workplace Bullying Is To Recognize It In The First Place

Like me, many people who are bullied are naive and believe that people are naturally good and would never intentionally set out to harm someone for no reason. This view is not only held by the naive; it is a view that is maintained by our society at large. We are constantly told to think positively and things will turn out just fine. That is good as far as it goes, but it fails to take into account that there are bad people with bad motives out there and the competitive and hierarchically structured workplace is a fertile breeding ground for these types of people. Failing to account for this fact dooms the naive target of a bully to months, if not years, of suffering as the abusive behavior continues unabated.

Whether it be the popular girl in high school or the CEO of a global corporation, it is my heartfelt belief that people who abuse the power of their positions will always win unless we train ourselves ahead of time to recognize them and learn effective combat strategies to use against them. Becoming a target of a person who is abusing his/her power to harm you is one the most stressful experiences any person can endure. It is definitely one of the most long lasting because bullies do not give up. They are relentless in their cruelty and abuse and the psychological effects their victims suffer do not go away easily.

It is also my belief that given the enormous toolkit of manipulative behaviors and psychological terror techniques available to these disordered personality types (which are getting larger each day with each new technology) passing laws to prevent the behavior is a futile strategy. Until humanity reaches a golden age where each individual human being sees the logic in treating others as they themselves would like to be treated, we will continue to have people who think and behave in a cruel manner while believing they are good. We will not change them. All we can change is ourselves. Therefore, our focus should be on giving individuals the knowledge they need to prevent their abusers from affecting their psyches. I did not have the knowledge to either recognize the abusive strategies as they were getting deployed against me nor was I able to escape the psychological toll they took on me.

I will limit my discussion about strategies for confronting workplace bullies to my experience with Rick and Stephanie. The mobbing added a whole other dimension that most cases of bullying never reach. Once it became a mobbing situation, there was little I could have done to change the outcome given that the full power and resources of the organization were working against me. So much time, money and human energy was wasted on destroying one human being's life – energy that could have been used for productive purposes and for the good of the company. After all, they could have gotten rid of the greedy and manipulative consulting company months earlier if they were not forced to wait out the statute of limitations for me to file a complaint. How many people did they have to lie to, how many lawyers did they have to pay for advice, how much time did they have to waste in investigation, how many resources did they have to dedicate to protecting themselves, how many people had to be transferred and/or taken off the project to reinforce the lies they propagated as defenses for Rick's negligence, how many IT resources were diverted to collecting emails, how much time and effort was spent reading and having to explain emails that implicated Rick and Stephanie's negligence and their own incompetence, how much attention was diverted from company business while they worried and stressed over being found out, how much was my reputation and character destroyed during and after the mobbing to support their lies, how much did these people cost the organization's bottom line on just this one case of their ineptitude, not to mention all the other cases they had to handle with HR over the years? Companies should start asking themselves these questions.

I have listed some of the quantifiable business costs of power abuse and harassment, but the business costs that cannot be quantified could be much higher. Companies must absorb the cost of retraining new employees when targets of abuse have the courage and wherewithal to leave. For those employees who decide the sue, the costs of defending a lawsuit can run into the thousands of dollars without even accounting for any favorable verdict or settlement costs. Employees who are subject to bullying type behaviors are under severe negative stress, which keeps them from focusing on the work at hand. Productivity is severely affected while the bullying boss concentrates on strategies for tormenting the target and the target is consumed with trying to figure out what to do to resolve the situation. In the short and long-term, it is the company that ultimately suffers the most, particularly if it decides to defend the harassing manager and keep him on the payroll. These kinds of managers are like serial killers in the sense that they strike over and over again. A company may think the problem is over once the target leaves its employ when, in reality, the problem has just begun. Keeping the power abuser on the payroll reinforces in his corrupt mind that his 'managerial style' is acceptable. It emboldens him to use the same manipulative, deceitful and cruel strategies on his next employee victim. The company can expect to have the problem repeated over and over again with each new employee until they are able to accept that the costs of getting rid of the real problem in the first place saves an organization all the costs associated with each new revolving door employee that the abuser chases off.

I believe the first step in combating workplace bullying is to recognize it in the first place. I gave a fairly detailed portrait of the methods Rick and Stephanie used to undermine me and my work. Although the methods that workplace power abusers employ may vary from case to case, most workplace bullying involves an abuse of power by a superior over a subordinate which does not usually stop until the target is eliminated or the power abuser is punished. The latter rarely happens because managers who abuse the power of their offices usually have plenty of allies in management and HR willing to line up behind them for support.

I think the imbalance in power, which is a hallmark of workplace bullying, makes it the corrosive problem it is. With HR almost always taking up arms with management and colleagues abandoning the target out of fear of becoming targets themselves, the victim is unfortunately left on her own most of the time. It is this sense of exclusion, isolation, abandonment and betrayal by people you have come to like and respect that leads to the helplessness and frustration so many targets feel. I not only lost hope, I became very frightened and the person I became most frightened of was my manager to whom I kept going for help but who failed to provide it at every turn. A working environment should never become a living nightmare and that is what it was for me.

There are many website and books on bullying and mobbing which provide a great deal of information about a bully's personality traits and motivations. I will not elaborate on them further except to say that bullies are illogical in every possible way. A lack of logical thought is intentional on their part and the sooner a target realizes this fact, the sooner she can take proactive steps to counter the attacks and do what she needs to do to protect herself, her health and her job, if possible. Don't waste time trying to figure out why they are doing what they are doing. If you find yourself the target of one of the these kinds of people, all you need to know is that anyone who is willing to employ bullying tactics to achieve their goals is cruel, manipulative and undeserving of any consideration. Period. Keeping that knowledge in the forefront of your mind will arm you in your uphill battle to keep your career intact and maintain your health and well being.

YOU should be your first priority at all times. Do not ever give into the temptation to cut your bully any slack. It will be difficult because it probably runs counter to everything you believe about empathy, cooperation and teamwork. But believe me when I tell you that this is the only way you will ever stand a chance at surviving and possibly even winning the battle. Targets cannot mount an effective counterattack unless their eyes are wide open to the reality of the world. Naivety needs go out the window and you need to start viewing human nature realistically. It is a sad state of affairs when I have to use warfare terminology to describe a relationship in the workplace, but combating a bullying boss is warfare. They are out to destroy you, your career and your reputation. If you make a tactical error in your plan of attack, it might just be the opening your bully needs to land the fatal blow.

Management knows how the game is played. They will continue to have the advantage until employers decide that these behaviors will not be tolerated under any circumstances. Until logic, freedom and the rights of all men and women of the world to not be abused are recognized, it is up to each target to shift the way they think about how the world works and prepare their minds to make sense out of the rabbit hole they find themselves falling into. I don't want anyone to ever have their reality altered to the point that they become a stranger to themselves.

I had no real knowledge of human nature because I had no real knowledge of myself. I was as ego-driven to self protect as they were which is why I lied when I told Lynette my husband and I were thinking about moving to Georgia and that I may have misunderstood Rick when he said I did not understand the change activities. My ego had me thinking I was the center of the universe and they would use my words as cover to investigate my claims. I was so self-centered it is sickening to me now. I actually thought I could manipulate events to work in my favor by lying. I did exactly what they were doing and all of us thought we were the good guys.

There are no good guys in these illusory, deceitful and corrupt environments we create for ourselves. There is only lunacy described as strategy. My ego guided all my actions as did their egos – even the writing of the letter to HR. It took me so long to be honest with myself about my motives, particularly when I was so consumed with hate for all of them. The fact is, none of us ever intentionally does what is bad for us. I wrote the letter because I was mad at Rick and at myself for leaving a job I loved for one that made me so miserable. I was not driven by a noble goal to save the project and help my fellow team members. I went to Vanessa and wrote the letter she requested me to write in order to help me. My ego had me thinking they would see what I saw about Rick and Mike's incompetence and do something about it. I would be the savior of the project by making it a more team-friendly environment. My naivety had me thinking I had the power to make change happen but in hierarchies, change does not happen unless and until the man at the top row thinks the change needs to be made. In that sense, I was in the wrong place at the wrong time because the man at the top of this hierarchy was willing to do absolutely anything to protect the interests of his hand-picked appointees serving as the gatekeepers in the rows below. Rick and Mike were two of those gatekeepers.

I cannot say I was the only naïve one in the bunch. We were all totally unaware of our true motivations except for the man who orchestrated everything with the legal help he got from his buddy, Ed. Those two men played us all. They even played Rick. The last week I was there, the CEO made himself a member of the committee overseeing the project so that he could appear to be its savior after I was gone. Rick was taken off the project once they were certain I wasn't going to sue and the consulting company was fired. Ed and his buddy set themselves up as the saviors of the situation and they were the only ones who were totally aware of what they were doing. No one was safe from them. We were all disposable because their powerful self interests hung in the balance. We were all just pieces on a game board that they set up for their own win and we all played our roles perfectly.

It could be said that I was completely ruined when I walked out of the building after leaving my badge with Kristine. I spent the subsequent years rebuilding my internal house and making it stronger. I have made the choice that I want to be a better person than I was before the bullying and mobbing and I am acquiring the mental tools I need to do that. I have learned that I can control my feelings and emotions and I don't always have to let them control me. There would have been enormous stress involved in what they did to me no matter what, but by crying I just fed into it and gave them added incentive to continue hurting me.

The only way a target will ever win is to be as aware of human nature and what motivates human beings to act as the abusers are. The CEO was intimately aware of what drove the minions below him because he made it his business to know. A power abuser will always make himself aware of human nature so that he can manipulate it in the best possible way. During one of our Christmas parties, the CEO stated that he has always been an ardent student and reader of history. Hitler was too. I would imagine most very powerful narcissists are fond of history because history gives them a window into the human soul. It clearly outlines strategies that have worked in the past and those that have not. History repeats itself not due to a lack of knowledge about it. History repeats itself because powerful interests find some benefit in having it repeat itself.

You don't fight fire with fire because you only get more fire. The puppets who the puppet master in my workplace were controlling so masterfully did not need the same knowledge of history he had to break free of his grip. They needed to be able to handle the truth. If just one of us had stepped away from our ego need to self protect in favor of pursuing truth, it would have been a game changer. Having a more realistic and truthful view of myself has also given me a more realistic and truthful view of other people. It might take time and effort, but the only way you will ever come out on top when dealing with power abusers like Marcus and Ed is to take care of your own soul first. Be stronger, be bolder, be wiser, have faith in an eternal power you can use to work for you, do the right thing no matter what, never give up truth, know that you have all the answers you need within you, trust yourself and no one else until they earn it, love yourself and know that when the stress gets to be absolutely unendurable and you think that you cannot make it another day – you can and will. There is no law in the world that will save you if you are up against people with the power to skirt the law or change the rules midstream in their favor. Therefore, you must learn to rely upon the universal laws of nature which depend upon reality and facts.

Every book, website, magazine and research paper on bullying offers different strategies for fighting bullying. I suppose it is good to be aware of all of them so you can make informed decisions, however; I have concluded that none of them would have helped me even if I had known about them. I know what I should have done and I would have known it then if I had been able to remain calm and unemotional. It still would have been an extremely tough battle and one I probably would have lost given the deck that was stacked against me, but at least I would have had pride in knowing that I gave them a run for their money. I would have left feeling good that I didn't give Rick and Stephanie the upper hand and that I told Kristine exactly what I thought of her instead of apologizing to her. When Ed, the chief ethics officer, asked me what the psychologist told me I would have told him what an incompetent weasel he was and that he was the one needing to see a therapist to figure out how he went so wrong in his life and job. When Vicky walked out of the conference room mad at me for questioning her motives, I would have let her continue walking and never looked back. I would have knocked on the door that last day on the job when Steve and Roberta were protecting themselves behind closed doors and told Steve that I had to talk to him. I would have asked Roberta point blank why she lied to the team leader overseas. Then I would have asked Steve what he did when he read the letter I wrote to HR. I wouldn't have couched my questions to Vanessa in hypotheticals. I would have told her straight up that Rick was harassing me and asked her why they were already coming up with defenses for a complaint I never filed. When Nicole sent me the email calling me a traitor with a smiley face next to it, I would have replied by calling her a two-faced coward with a frowny face next to it. I would have faced the very difficult fact that I was on my own, as most targets are when it comes to power abusing behavior. Other people can certainly offer advice, try to intervene or help you come up with a solution but in the final analysis, it all comes down to just you and the actions you take that will determine whether you overcome the experience with no regrets and with your emotional, mental and physical well being intact.

These are the regrets I have - that I didn't stand up to their lies and character assassination. I should have countered everything they said and confronted them boldly. They had the power of their positions and organization, but I had the power of the truth. I could have left there with my pride intact, knowing that I made them know I wasn't the stupid little communications specialist they thought I was.

Although there are some strategies targets can employ if they decide they do not want to put up with the abuse and determine they have the strength and composure to combat it, I thought long and hard about providing those strategies in this book because I know the emotional devastation that power abusing bully types can inflict. It can become even worse when the target tries to assert her right to be treated with the respect and dignity deserving of all human beings. Given the current state of affairs in many American workplaces, my strategies are extremely difficult to follow. Until we come to an understanding as a society that we will not tolerate, condone or encourage this kind of behavior in any setting – be it a workplace, school or home; then each of us individually will have to chart our own course if we find ourselves targeted. I want all targets to be able to do this consciously and with their eyes wide open to the dangers involved in any strategy they decide to employ.

Survival Of The Fittest

Once you find yourself under the authority of a corrupt person or persons you have to leap into survival mode. In survival environments, there is no room for engagement, fulfillment, teamwork, open communication, respect, or any of the other qualities that define a human consciousness whose aim is to grow and nurture its talents and knowledge. The values posted throughout the building and the mission statement printed on your business card become mere platitudes that will lead to your destruction if internalized. You need to put them on the back burner when dealing with your abuser. Your new set of values will include a heightened knowledge of human nature, a calm demeanor, a mindful sizing up of the environment for purposes of creating a strategy, a banishment of denial, a reliance on facts (truth) and a steel-like armor of confidence in yourself that can withstand the underhanded and manipulative assaults against your consciousness.

Whether you like it or not, you have entered a war that has been declared against you and the only way for you to win this war is to face the fact that the more powerful side in a war will always win unless the less powerful side can come up with a strategy that exploits the weaknesses in their enemy and the strengths in themselves. Your biggest strength is knowing that you were targeted for a reason and that anyone who targets another human being for destruction will use any and all behaviors to make certain they accomplish their goal. Deceit, back door deals, manipulation of facts and all the other behaviors I have outlined in my own story are the toolkit of a power abuser. No lie is outlandish enough and no behavior shameful enough because they have the power to turn the lie into truth, the shame into self-righteousness; and the illusion of their own mind's making that you are the enemy into the reality on the ground. It is a strategy used by all war mongers - make your enemies into sub-humans who do not deserve dignity or respect and you will be able to get people to follow you into hell under the banner that they are doing the right thing.

The person out to destroy your job and career is a war monger at the level of one. Therefore, the experts in war provide targets with some very good strategies for forging a counterattack. I have extracted some of those strategies from *The U.S. Army Survival Manual* and have put them in the context of a workplace whose values and mission have been supplanted by amoral people who have personal agendas they are willing to carry out by any and all means.[10] I will review some of those tips here.

Size Up The Situation

Know thyself is an ancient Greek saying that Plato used repeatedly in his writings. I think it is because it is only by knowing oneself that one can know anyone else. We are all cut from the same cloth. We all have the same human needs and desires. Understanding the commonality of the human soul allows us to size up situations and people realistically – not how we want them to be or wish them to be. My lack of understanding of myself and my environment led to my lack of understanding of everyone else. I was so totally me-centered in terms of my own self interests that it left me totally clueless about everyone else who was likewise me-centered in terms of their own self interests. We were all driven by the same motive to self-protect yet had no awareness of our motive. It was natural we would all collide with one another while pursuing actions we perceived protected our individual interests.

I would encourage all targets to be aware of this very strong and overriding motive of all human beings to self-protect because it will allow them to accurately size up most competitive workplaces. As a whole, human beings are animals who have not yet been able to shed their animal consciousness because it is beneficial to them to keep it in animal-style hierarchies of power. Values like open communication, honesty, respect for all individuals and personal integrity belong to a human consciousness that realizes its true nature. They are the hallmarks of a person who has taken the time to *know thyself*. They define a human character guided by the truth within and not by motives created by external people and structures which have the power to weaken us by tempting us to conform to something less. Until a person's actions prove they have a strong character, then assume they do not. Do not assume the values the company espouses are the same values your boss holds. More often, they are not and when they are not, then the boss usually rules because that is the nature of the modern-day workplace. HR protects the boss because they are operating under the same understanding of the law that Ed had which says that protecting the boss equates to protecting the company since your boss is an agent of the company. That is where our 'rule of law' has taken us and it is something all targets should understand in order to properly size up their situation.

I did not properly size up the situation. Truth is very hard for anyone to take but for someone as ego-driven and desirous of self-glorification as Rick was, it is impossible to take. In my anger, I let it all hang loose in the letter I wrote to HR. I should have reviewed the letter through Rick's eyes before sending it. If I had, I would have seen how it could be perceived as an attack on him personally. I should have taken a step back and allowed some time to pass before composing it. With some time to cool down, I may have decided to take Vicky's advice and not go to HR at all. I may have decided to concentrate on the work Lynette was giving me and focus on school. I may have decided that a crappy job was better than no job at all; which is what I should have expected when I bucked the power structure of the male-dominated company I worked in.

Although I would not change anything now because of the knowledge I have gained through the experience and the growth I have undergone as a human being, I would advise all truth tellers and change agents out there to carefully size up their own situations and determine all human factors involved before they begin bucking their own power structures. Do not forge any strategy out of anger. Forge it because you believe in the worth of your cause. If change is not value driven, then it is not the kind of change worth believing in. I was not values-driven when I wrote the letter to HR as I have tried so hard to make myself believe. I was self-driven and in my selfishness, I damaged Rick's core. He was not the kind of person who is strong enough to take the unvarnished truth without lashing back. I was not the kind of person who was strong enough to take the abuse he and his buddies dished out in retaliation. I should have known that going in.

Don't Act Hastily In The Heat Of The Moment

When I was walking to the other building with Vicky telling her she was in the cat bird's seat, I had no idea I would find myself staring at Rick and Stephanie in the meeting. It was something I did on the spot without thinking about it. By hastily deciding to stare at them in the spur of the moment, I gave the enemy a two-fold win. Not only did I give them a valid excuse to terminate my employment, I gave them the core of their strategy to paint me as unbalanced when I quit and they were facing a constructive discharge lawsuit. Constructive discharge is when working conditions become so intolerable as to amount to a firing, despite a lack of a formal termination notice. The fact that I went to my manager over and over again about Rick <u>and</u> I went to Vanessa my last day satisfied the notice requirement that my employer was aware of the conditions and did nothing. Painting me as unbalanced and dangerous would have negated any such claim. I gave them the ammunition they needed when I chose to stare at Stephanie and Rick, stupidly thinking that Mike had my back.

It was a disastrous move on my part to stare at Stephanie and Rick and it was the result of over confidence in my position after talking to Mike and having him tell me they would give Rick "team coaching lessons." Overconfidence in your own position can lead you to make a critical error like I did with the staring incident. The only way to ensure you do not fall into that trap is to never let go of your own value system. The critical rule you must follow is the golden rule. Never do unto others as you would not like done unto you. No matter how atrocious their lies get, how outlandish their behavior becomes or how flagrant the corruption is, never let yourself stoop to combating them with the same behaviors and strategies because you will most certainly lose the battle and the war. You must view the entire experience through the lens of truth - the truth about people, the truth about your environment and the truth about yourself. It is essential that this work be done beforehand though. You must create a strong character first in order to be able to be strategic in your approach towards the enemy in your workplace because they will use your faults and weaknesses against you.

As hard as I tried with my apologies to Mike and Kristine, there was no retreat from the staring incident. Wrong is wrong and that was very wrong. Mike's false assertion that time heals all wounds and Kristine's pretension that I would be returning to her team instead of getting fired does not make it any less wrong. Regardless of what they were doing and saying to me to keep me from going to HR, I actually gave them a valid reason for terminating my employment and all the excuses in the world do not change that fact. We must all take responsibility for our actions no matter how entitled we believe we are to act in ways that are wrong.

Rely On Your Own Internal Sense Of Direction To Guide You

I was always going to Vicky for advice and the advice she was giving me was coming directly from the mouth of the enemy. By refusing to face the truth right in front of me and preferring to listen to Vicky, I let them manipulate me until they could come up with a valid reason to terminate my employment.

Rick and Stephanie were obvious enemies but when conditions started to become surreal, I should have realized there were powerful enemies lurking in the background. Kristine told me as much when I went to her after Rick accused me of not understanding the change activities. She told me I was dealing with power and needed to go back and apologize to him. I thought Rick was the power she was referring to but I should have realized it went much higher when all my pleas for help were going unanswered and Mike did his about-face after our meeting. These were, after all, managerial bureaucrats I was dealing with - not creative geniuses accustomed to breaking all the rules. They would never, ever have put their jobs on the line with all their lies and manipulations if they did not know their backs were covered by someone with the power to cover them.

Overcome Fear And Panic

If I can get you, the reader, to listen to any piece of advice I am giving; then please, please take this one to heart. Fear and panic supplant the protection a rational human mind provides. Your imagination takes over and conjures up all kinds of scenarios not based on anything except paranoia and the belief that the worst will happen to you if you do not take matters into your own hands and manipulate them in your favor. In cases of imbalances of power, the control will always be in the hands of the more powerful because they control the information.

I have no idea what they told my manager. I have no idea what was told to Vicky, Vanessa, Lynette or anyone else who abandoned me and left me alone with only my fear and paranoia to guide me. The people at the top of the hierarchy are shape changers who can change the narrative any way they want and choose what will be told to anyone. Keeping control of the narrative in the hands of the few at the top of the hierarchy is at the core of the whole " on a need to know basis" of the hierarchical structure. The CEO and ethics officer of this corporation decided to back Rick because their own self-interests relied on backing him. By ignoring the letter I wrote to HR and the concerns of the other team members that were voiced to Vanessa, they put themselves in a vulnerable position. I am certain Rick never told them about the action plan he and Stephanie ignored. They probably didn't know anything about it or about Rick's efforts to cover it up until they began reviewing the emails in preparation for their defense of a lawsuit that never came. They dug themselves deeper and deeper into a hole by choosing to protect him and themselves. That is why the behavior and lies became so outrageous. I blamed myself for so long for being weak but I believe it would have been difficult for anyone to be strong when a pack of scared people with an animal consciousness to self protect descends on them. The pack is out for nothing less than the kill. The only way to protect yourself is to create a grounded human consciousness in advance that is aware that such a reality can exist when a person at the top of a hierarchy feels threatened and all he has is a strong ego to guide him, along with an army of hand-picked appointees who are willing to do whatever he says in order to protect their own self interests.

You cannot imagine the level of fear and paranoia that arises in the human mind when a person is operating alone within a cohesive system of people out to get them. Peer pressure is nothing compared to a power structure that is garnering all its resources against you and has been successful in isolating you. All you have available to guide you is your own inner core. If you let it become overwhelmed with the stresses of the situation, which is so much easier said than done, then you will most certainly lose.

I watched a news program where a young girl admitted to killing a toddler in a daycare because after a grilling by the police where she was told she could go home if she would confess, she confessed to a crime she claims not to have committed. The evidence presented on the show makes me believe she is telling the truth. Unfortunately, she is telling the truth from behind prison walls after getting convicted of the crime. Her life as she knew it is over forever. Her legacy is forever changed and her destiny on this earth derailed because she bet against the truth in that interrogation room based on the false promise of someone who was providing her with false information.

In these kinds of situations, the interrogators create circumstances where they are the enemy and savior at the same time. They tell the person they have certain evidence that will put the person away for years but if they confess, then they can work with them for a better outcome. Unless the person has an extremely strong inner core and value system, or alternatively a lawyer advising him, then they can very easily fall into the good cop/bad cop scenario that has been set up to trap them. The fear of what may befall them if they do not take the interrogators up on their offer for a better outcome has created many a false confession in the heat of the moment where the mind of the interrogated is running wild with worst case scenarios.

I believe the executive enforcers in my workplace were setting up the same kind of good cop/bad cop scenario acting as enemy and savior at the same time when they had Mike meet with me to give me false assurances that he would take my advice to heart and give Rick team coaching lessons. Although he was just as deficient in his team building abilities, the offer was a false one. His sole motive for making such assurances was to keep me from going to Steve as I told Rick I wanted to do in our conference room meeting. It was their insurance policy that I would not go to HR before they could terminate my employment the following Monday based on Rick's lie to Kristine that I was insubordinate with him. Apparently, Kristine and Vicky were not judged worthy of needing to know about this insurance policy and it is why they were both asking me if I was okay – if I wanted to talk after my meeting with Mike. They thought he was there to terminate me, not offer his false promises of help.

On Tuesday of my final week there, I wrote an email to Mike telling him I was sorry for my outburst and would work with Rick and Kristine to do whatever I needed to do to make things work out. He never responded to me (of course) but I remember that the night before writing it, the stress had become unbearable. I recall sitting on the floor of my bedroom trying to figure out what I should do. I was beginning to become frantic and wondering who I could trust. Was Mike in on it? If so, I should do this; but if not then this, but then again if I do that then what? Questions and scenarios were going round and round in my head. I didn't know where to turn or what to do. I was completely alone. My husband wasn't there to clarify things for me and I was becoming very scared. Sleep was non-existent and if I did happen to doze off, I would wake up with my teeth clenched down so hard my jaw hurt.

To prevent the kind of fear and panic that was causing me to unravel, a target needs to learn the Buddhist art of letting go. I was so desperate to keep my job at this company that I literally let myself go stark raving mad. I let myself become so attached to my job because I was not attached to anything else in my life. I had no hobbies, no real marriage and no real friends. The only thing I valued was my son and he was growing up and away from me. I loved working in communications for this company and the thought that I was losing the one thing I was passionate about was unbearable to me. Facing the possibility that I was losing something I loved so much was creating fear and panic on a massive scale. A strong attachment to anything in life will create panic and fear at the thought of losing it, whether it be a job, money, spouse, child, home, boyfriend ... whatever. It is good to value people and possessions but when it gets to the point that you cannot imagine life without them, then you have entered a danger zone and should begin reevaluating the relationship you have with the person or thing you feel so attached to.

Attachment places happiness outside yourself in a person or thing. If happiness is outside of you, then you must accept that pain is as well. You make yourself vulnerable to self-pity, depression, rage, jealousy, anger, anxiety, fear, panic and all the other negative emotions one feels when things in the external environment are not going so well. I gave the perpetrators of the mobbing power over my life by giving them control over my happiness and pain. If I had not let my job become the center of my universe, then there would have been nothing to fear when I saw it slipping away. I would have moved on of my own accord without ever looking back. It would have just become another experience in the ever-expanding universe of experiences contained within a human life.

Improvise

The free online dictionary defines improvisation as the ability to perform or make quickly from materials and sources available without previous planning. Improvisation may end up being the only strategy a target is left with when trying to navigate through the obstacle course of manipulations and lies created by worm-like, amoral, power abusers who are willing to say and do anything to protect their turf and carry out their personal agendas. The are no company policy manuals to help you plan your next move under such circumstances. You are on your own. Creating your own strong sense of self based upon a realistic view of human nature is crucial to your personal survival and well-being in corrupt environments where truth, reason and logic are decimated so that the deceitful, insecure and ego-driven power players can achieve their win.

It is extremely difficult to think, much less act, when it gets to the point of mobbing. I was unable to focus on anything at that point. As the bully spreads lies about your work to other people in management, they begin to believe him and you lose credibility by the day. Your colleagues disappear and your support system completely breaks down. Through their conscious motive to completely isolate you as the loser and loner, it becomes very easy to doubt yourself and your position. The tendency is to retreat inward and completely disengage. The Army refers to this as "passive outlook." Passive outlook is when lethargy, mental numbness and indifference creep into your mental processes and leave you feeling hopeless and helpless. This phenomenon of passive outlook is the enemy's best friend. It allows them to call the target of their campaign unsocial, unmotivated, unskilled, unwilling to learn and incapable of doing the job they have been given. From the tidbits of information Vicky teased me with, I have concluded these were the kinds of adjectives Rick and Stephanie were using to describe me in their behind-the-scenes campaign to demean my character and make me out to be an incompetent trouble-maker.

Improvisation is an art. It is not easy. It requires a great deal of confidence in your ability to act on the spot. Hindsight is 20/20 but as I look back, there were some actions I could have taken to at least contain Rick and Stephanie's ability to ruin my reputation behind the scenes. With the hope that it will give others who find themselves in this evil catch-22, I will list some of the actions I should have taken to contain the damage done to me but I would emphasize that all these actions required me to remain calm – a quality I was finding in short supply at the time.

> 1. When Stephanie ripped the presentation apart, I would have requested she stay put while I printed out a copy of the script for the two of us to go over. If she said she had a meeting to go to or a telephone call to take, I would have rescheduled the meeting to go over the presentation. I would not have created a new presentation with her templates. Instead, I would have made her work with me to change the one I had already prepared no matter how many meetings it took.

> 2. After we finished revising it, I would have then requested a meeting with Kristine to have her go over it with Stephanie, Rick and me, since Rick seemed to trust her judgment so much.

> 3. I would have asked that Steve Argon attend the sham meeting with Rick, Kristine and me since they were discussing what I would be doing upon my return to HR. That would only be logical since he was the one concerned about headcount. If they said he was unavailable, I would have asked that it be rescheduled.

> 4. I would have countered every one of Vicky's false

assertions with the truth as I saw it. I let her manipulate me out of a false sense of niceness. I would not have been "nice" to any of them. They did not deserve it. I would have seen her and Nicole for the cowards they are and found the strength within myself to stand alone.

5. I would have countered all of Rick's emails. It would have given me great pleasure to point out what a fool he was when he tried coming off as the communications expert.

6. I would have rescheduled the meeting with Rick and Stephanie when she left early and Rick asked me to come up with a set of questions for her. We would have sat down and written out all the change activities together so that he would never have been able to lie to my face about not understanding them.

7. I would have asked Stephanie how I was going to come up with dates for the communication plan when I had never done an implementation before and could not do it without her input. Then I would have insisted she sit down with me so we could come up with the dates together.

8. I would have continued sending emails to Rick and Stephanie until I got answers to mine.

9. I would have walked over to Kristine's cubicle and insisted she tell me what Rick told her in their afternoon meeting that later became "the work plan meeting."

10. I would have made an appointment to talk to Steve, since he never thought it worthwhile to talk to me.

11. I would have gone to the CEO, who was Ed's direct supervisor, although I suspect he knew as much as Ed did. I would not have left any stone unturned in an effort to get justice.

12. I would have trusted my instincts about Kristine, particularly since Lynette told me no one liked her in the office overseas, and I would have judged her actions accordingly. If I had done so, I would not have been so blind-sided by her betrayal and would have told her she was the

crazy one for referring me to a psychiatrist when my reaction to her outrageous lies and pretense was a perfectly normal reaction under the circumstances.

There are many other actions I could have taken as well, but you get the picture. The reason I never did these things is because I was in a fog of unreality. I kept thinking someone would come to my rescue (as Mike pretended to do) because they liked me and knew what a good worker I was. It never occurred to me that they were all self-absorbed in protecting their own turf. I really thought Vicky was my friend, Kristine was looking out for me and Vanessa's priority was taking care of the employees who came to her with their problems. Their true motivations were on display, I just refused to see them. I didn't have my eyes open. It was easier for me to cry and wish things would change by playing to people's compassion. Unfortunately for me, these people had no compassion. They were out for the kill. Instead of playing to their compassion, my tears satisfied their sick desire for revenge.

Taking an offensive posture with these actions would have required me to be an extremely strong person who was able to stand up to immoral and corrupt authority in every sense of the word because these were all executives, vice presidents and managers forging this mobbing. The intimidation factor is huge when the power is so unbalanced. My own manager was a pitiful excuse for one. She compensated for her cowardice with an irrational bitterness and resentment towards me for causing her such trouble. This is how incompetent people without scruples turn the tables on their targets. Then, in the email exchange with Vicky many months later when I realized what was done to me, they all stayed true to the form of their weak characters and blamed my manager's actions on her culture; telling me that in her culture people do not feel comfortable confronting others. If that is her culture, she should never have been appointed a director of an American subsidiary. The fact is, it is not her culture. People like this manager are extremely inventive in coming up with excuses for their personal and professional failures. The ego is a very powerful force and is the major factor that prevents most of us from doing the kind of self-examination we should constantly be doing. We simply do not want to admit our own shortcomings and we do not want anyone else pointing them out to us either.

For myself, I let my emotions completely overwhelm me. It was a time for analysis and I was incapable of it. The stress was simply unbearable and there was no relief from it because the players in the mobbing didn't want to provide any relief to me. The ball was always in their court because that is how the game is played. If this book accomplishes anything, I want to make people aware of this phenomenon so that as the signs begin appearing in their own lives, a light bulb will go off and they will realize the reality of what is happening before it is too late for their emotional and psychological well being.

I cannot emphasize enough how important it is to try control your emotions and level of stress. It is a gargantuan effort when a target is undergoing the experience, but being aware of the reality of what it happening is half the battle. In reading over the first chapter of this book, I noticed how much I talked about how the two bully bosses 'made me feel'. Their goal is to make you feel like you are not up to the job by making you question yourself and your abilities. Bullies are masters of manipulation. They will use their toolkit of deceptions, lies, evasions and false accusations to keep you off balance. No one deserves to be treated this way. You must always remember that they are the inadequate ones and your main goal should always be to maintain your confidence and composure until you are able to find a solution, even if it means giving up the job you love and transferring to another department, finding another job or quitting. You cannot find the proper balance between listening to your intuition and using your logical reasoning capabilities to combat the bully if you let stress and other factors keep you unfocused and confused.

When I enter a workplace now, I do not go into the job thinking that it is going to be an environment of teamwork and cooperation. I start with the assumption that everyone is out for themselves until they prove otherwise. This is the only way to be until the workplace culture shifts. Thinking this way does not change you or your humanity. You can still be the person you strive to be. You can be even better because you are no longer dealing with the naivety that works against all targets. That is your real enemy because it blinds you to the truth.

I feel strongly that I would be remiss if I did not point out that improvisation and fearlessness can get you so far before the best strategy is to just get away from the situation completely without looking back. There are certain people who are capable of committing the most horrific acts against humanity without feeling anything at all. Nothing. They are the psychopaths and sociopaths of this world; many of whom are masquerading as executives, managers and supervisors in the halls of our corporations, governments, schools, churches, hospitals, law offices and other organizations. They assume the cover of normalcy, but that is far from the reality. Psychopathy and sociopathy are synonymous terms for all intent and purposes and equally scary in that the dominant characteristic of both conditions is a lack of conscience. A sociopath or psychopath does not have any moral compass whatsoever. The common perception is that all psychopaths are criminals. This is not true. They are our spouses, bosses, neighbors and friends. They are also the most evil people walking the planet and according to most psychiatrists they cannot be cured. No one is safe from them because they hide behind a mask of compassion, charm, wit, culture, education, and social status. The scary part is that they do not possess these traits. They play at them. They learn at a very early age that they are a different kind of human being. They do not feel the same emotions as we do and without a sense of right and wrong because of their inability to analyze themselves honestly, they are capable of doing anything to anyone.

Sociopaths are usually of average intelligence but they feel superior to us mere mortals. We are restrained in what we will consider doing because of our sense of right and wrong. Psychopaths view that as weakness. They have no such restraints and they will lie, manipulate, undermine, harm and destroy anyone to achieve their personal agendas. According to Dr. Robert Hare, an expert in the field of psychopathy, a psychopath will not feel embarrassed or guilty when caught in a lie. They simply change the facts to suit the lie. They have become adept at rationalizing everything they do, so that even their most heinous acts seem reasonable in their minds. More often than not, their rationalizations convince them they are benefiting the organizations they work for and society as whole. They are emotionless people incapable of taking other people into consideration as they cause personal devastation all around them.

If you suspect your bully falls into this class of human, you will never win. Get out and away from them as quickly as possible because they will do absolutely anything in their power to destroy you and since their charming disguise has probably won over everyone else in management who would be able to help you, you are out there on your own. I have a feeling that even if I had incorporated all the strategies I just outlined I would have ended up doing exactly as I did. I walked out on the career I loved when that was the only personal choice I had left after having the ethics officer and general counsel accuse me of mental instability. He was the second in charge who reported directly to the outwardly charming CEO perched at the top of this subsidiary's hierarchy. The ethics officer of this large corporation would not have handled my phone call to him so callously if he had not had the tacit approval of the first in charge. I was trapped from the top down and exiting the scene of the crime was the best strategy available to me. The decision was heart wrenching and will forever affect my life but I do believe it was the only decision I could have made that would keep my life on the correct trajectory and lead me to my ultimate destiny without harm to myself or anyone else.

Live By Your Values

This ties back to not acting hastily in the heat of the moment. If I had had a clear set of personal principles over and above the values of the company, they would have served as my guide through the very turbulent waters of a workplace whose cowardly power structure wanted me gone for their own gain. I would not have acted like a coward myself by bullying Rick and Stephanie with my staring at them. Value living would have kept me balanced and focused on my own soul and mind. I would have been the responsible adult who does not allow herself to stoop to the level of liars, bullies and cowards. If I had not eventually gained that set of values for myself, which I have based on the Bible's Ten Commandments, I would have continued to view myself as the victim who has every right to hate and blame them for what they did.

For targets of bullying and mobbing behaviors, I would say trust your instincts. Remain calm through every situation. Never doubt yourself. Get advice from others but don't rely on others to make your decisions for you. Know that no job is worth losing your integrity over and no friend who asks you to act against your better judgment is worth having. Realize that no situation ever lasts forever and we should use each one as a learning experience to help us grow into the people we are meant to become. Never do anything that harms your soul or that of a fellow human being. Remember what your mother told you — that things always look better in the morning (because they do). Try new things and do only what makes you happy. You will come out the other side stronger and wiser and happier. Count on it!

Act Like The Natives Who Have Adapted To Their Environment

This is tricky. Adapting to a strange physical environment includes dressing like the natives, following the customs of the natives and generally blending in until you are able to get out. I may have been able to follow this strategy if I had known the real rules of the corrupt workplace I was in but I did not because they were unwritten. Taking this company's values at face value was dangerous in terms of a subordinate's career and well being. I do not know how these unwritten rules came about or the strategy of the company in having two sets of rules — one for the managers and one for the other employees, but this situation usually occurs in hierarchical organizations when there is a leader at the top who has an agenda in conflict with the stated mission and values of the organization. Since there is no one more powerful to keep him/her in check and no managers on the rows below with any incentive to keep the power in check because they have been hired or appointed to their positions by the person at the top of the pyramid, this leader of the pack rules and the unwritten rules become law.

When the official HR policy manuals, mission statements and values of your organization appear to be non-existent, then you must assume they have been supplanted by rules and values that protect a certain person or persons within the organization. In hierarchical organizations, the only persons with the power to supplant the values and rules are the people occupying the top row of the hierarchy. Given that most targets are on the bottom rungs of the hierarchy and answerable to the power structure at the top, they are the ones who will lose in any power struggle unless they arm themselves with an ability to face the truth that their egos deny them. In corrupt environments, people at the bottom rungs are not important. They are not valued. They are not essential to the organization. They are merely tools that can be replaced by other tools and expensed on the balance sheet of accountability. When the shit storm of a scandal or lawsuit hits the fan, they are the ones who will get caught downwind. These are hard truths for most of us to face but it is reality nonetheless.

The general counsel who served as the chief ethics officer at the company where I was mobbed provides a stark illustration of what happens in environments where the rules and values have been supplanted by the rules and self interests of the people in charge. There was an incident that happened while I worked for him that gave me a great deal of insight into the state of his consciousness. He was in charge of putting together the notebooks for the quarterly board meetings and he had to work very closely with the accounting department for all the financial information. The vice president of accounting at the time had been with the company for years and was very passionate in his loyalty to it. The general counsel had been there for less than two years but had formed a very close bond with the CEO who hired him. Apparently the general counsel had a disagreement with the accounting VP or had done something that the VP didn't like. Either way, the VP came to his office one morning and began yelling at him using a couple of choice words on his way into his office and behind closed doors. The CEO's secretary sat next to me and we both looked at one another knowing that something was going to hit the fan. The vice president of accounting left the general counsel's office after just a couple of minutes and the general counsel followed him out the door and headed straight to human resources. The next day, or a couple of days thereafter, this very passionate VP of accounting came by my desk and apologized for his language and behavior. He then went to the CEO's secretary and apologized to her as well. The secretary and I were both rather surprised that he apologized to us since it wasn't us with whom he had a problem. After telling my husband about it, we both concluded that there were other forces at work and they had nothing to do with the secretary or me. The general counsel used the power of his office and his influence with the CEO and the vice president of human resources to humiliate this VP for bruising his ego in front of observers (the secretary and me). It was not enough for him to work out his differences with this VP in private, he had to teach him a lesson and show him his real place in the hierarchy under its new leadership. It couldn't have been more than a couple of months before the VP retired and a new VP of accounting took his place.

At the time this incident occurred, I had no idea about how the hierarchy of office politics worked. That may sound like a naive position and I now know I was naive, but it was a naivety that they intentionally fostered by lying to employees and telling them they welcomed transparency and open, face-to-face communication. Corrupt power structures thrive on this kind of naive stupidity to function. It helps them siphon off the dissidents, troublemakers, truth tellers and potential leaders of conscience. They want to know who will play the game and who won't. When I disappeared from the workplace without a trace, I know people talked. Some learned the truth and some didn't. For the ones who learned the truth, they had new knowledge and could decide to conform or not. For the ones who conformed, the corporation came that much closer to a complete standstill in terms of growth and prosperity in the form of innovation – an area the egoistic managers would be very uncomfortable in. The ones who didn't learn the truth were still in peril and faced the prospect of having their own heads chopped off if they reared them by speaking the truth boldly and transparently.

It hurt me when Kristine told me in one of my yearly reviews that I was not the kind of manager the company looked for but after years of soul searching, I cannot help but conclude she was right. I would never have wanted to act like the natives in that company. I never want to do what she, Vicky, Vanessa, Roberta and Nicole did to keep their jobs and careers. I see the corrupt patterns of that workplace repeated over and over again at the minimum wage, temp jobs I have been working. My colleagues think their opinions and feelings matter because they are told by the corporations they matter. When I see them go to the managers to voice their complaints, it is always like deja vu all over again. The managers pretend to listen to them, but nothing changes. They get more and more frustrated and outspoken and soon become viewed as the trouble makers on the team.

I keep my mouth shut when it comes to voicing my own opinions to management but I do not keep my mouth shut with regard to my colleagues. I tell them my story with the hope that my experience will become one more piece of information in their own mind's bank of information and they will incorporate it when making any decisions with regard to their jobs and long-term employment future. I do not want anyone to ever undergo an experience like mine if I can prevent it by giving them another perspective besides the one the corporation is spoon feeding them. I want them to incorporate the truth in their thinking in order to come up with the proper strategy to protect themselves and ensure their emotional, mental and financial longevity.

The voice that was once silenced and made unable to even read about bullying will be silenced no more. I will speak loud and I will speak as clearly as I can to untangle the web of lies that we have been told in order to create the upside-down world so many of us must now navigate in. I will protect my own soul as much as I can while trying to protect the souls of my fellow men and women with whom I come into contact in my daily life.

Listen To Your Intuition But Don't Forget To Apply Basic Skills

I was totally unprepared in handling Stephanie and Rick. I did not know that people like them existed, especially in the company where I was working. You can never lose sight that bullies are people and bullying behavior is behavior learned early in life. Rick was not only willing to sacrifice me to achieve his goals, he was willing to sacrifice his accomplices as well. He had everyone fooled. I wasted so much time wondering how he could be so stupid when I was the stupid one for underestimating Stephanie and him. Once a target suspects he is being undermined by recognizing some of the signs of bullying like knit picking, overwork or under-work, non-responsiveness, the providing of insufficient or wrong instruction, exclusion, having areas of responsibility removed, belittlement or the host of other manipulations bullies use; then it's time to leap into action. Do not waste one second trying to figure out why this person is acting this way. It is wasted effort that can be better used cultivating a strategy and state of mind to protect yourself.

My story is simply a microcosm of why we have remained blind to these strategies and continue to let them be used by politicians, government officials, businessmen, parents and even religious leaders the world over. They serve to benefit people with power who are willing to abuse that power in order to benefit themselves and/or their agendas. We can pass all the laws in the world, which these power players are more than happy to do in order to appease us because they know there is always a way to get around the laws they pass without any negative consequences befalling them. They are, after all, the enforcers of the laws they pass. They can always find some reason to harass an innocent victim they want to arrest. They can always exchange favors with their colleagues in power to cover up wrongdoing. They can always lie for each other knowing the favor will be returned.

As much as we might like to think that passing laws against

bullying will stem the flow of this behavior, we are only fooling ourselves. I was protected by laws as are many victims of bullying and mobbing. These managers knew it and so I ended up suffering a fate far worse than if there were no laws in effect to specially protect me. We no longer talk in language of truth, justice and fairness when it comes to the American workplace. When I read blogs and Facebook posts on bullying, the advice is never that American management and HR practices are fair, legal and rational and employees will be treated fairly when they try to get assistance and relief from a boss that is abusive. No. It is all about how they need to protect themselves from the hit men in the HR department who will lie, cheat, manipulate and threaten them in order to protect the abusive superior. A typical example is given in the following string of advice that was given to an employee on Facebook who said she went to a supervisor to express some concerns that she and some of her co-workers had about the hostile work environment they were in. The supervisor went to the employee's director, who then arranged for a meeting the next morning to which only this employee was invited. When she asked her supervisor if all the other employees would be there, she was told "yes" but when she checked with the employees directly, they said they had not received invitations. Some of the comments included:

- I would forward email and tell coworkers to be there. Hopefully you have coworkers that will stand with you.....

- Be prepare to be terminated. Get your ducks line up. Send the emails home and whatever else you will need for lawsuit.

- Start looking for another job just in case someone is trying to set you up to get fired.

- Your instincts are right. This is a set up! Tell them you will not attend and wait until another meeting is called with all employees being invited. Contact your union rep if you have one.

- Document and see if you can get your co-workers to document that they have not been invited. If you do decide to attend, bring a tape recorder and be sure that you said on recording that you were under the impression that all were invited but had confirmed with others that they were not invited as of this time, less than 24 hours prior to the meeting. Start all of this now.

- I was in a similar situation. You could refuse to "meet" unless you have representation or your coworkers present.

- Write down every single thing you can in the time you have left that has led up to this very moment that has to do with this meeting tomorrow. When you get home, or somewhere out of the office, send it to your own personal email address, one that is your own, not affiliated with your job.

- Make notes of you attending the meeting if no one else was invited but told they were. Make copies of your emails and use a log on dates and times when you met with your supervisors. If all plays in favor for everyone but you, than you at least have evidence that you were working towards resolving the problem through proper communication and was never told how to handle the situation otherwise. Also, if things get really heated, you may have evidence to present in case of wrongful termination, discrimination, or negligence. Either way, cover your own butt, and don't trust that they are playing by the rules.

- Get an attorney.

- Call in sick. Go to the doctor or get a doctor's note and go out on FMLA.

- Set up! Log everything, even your discussions with your supervisor. Be careful of your co-workers possible back stabbers.

- If you think an audio recorder will not be allowed, just bring one without announcing it first and let everybody know that the meeting is being recorded. If they balk, then indicate that you will be taking notes as well.

- Take witness / union rep. Stay calm.

- Agree with all of the above Print out emails, any documents, delete things you should and bring in a tape recorder and turn it on and make sure you have their consent to record and then show them the email that all were invited and see what they say. Sounds like you need a new job. Hard to come by I know but keep trying and keep your head up.

- This sounds like the classic ambush meeting. I was terminated two months ago using this method. Go in early so you can clean out emails and documents. If this an ambush- they will disable your account. Do not sign anything. I told my former employer I needed to meet with an attorney before I decided what terms I would agree to. Good luck with everything.

- Bring everybody. At least one to be a witness. Be prepared to have a constructive conversation. Bring paper and pen to take notes.

- If you are not allowed to bring anyone else to the meeting, then don't go. They cannot force you to.

- Call your local police dept about legality on recorder.

If one takes an objective look at the advice this employee was given, it is really rather scary. However, it provides a stark example of how totally irrational human resources departments have become and of how deep the mistrust in them runs. What have human resources departments morphed into that an employee who brings up a legitimate concern that she and her colleagues have is suddenly having to worry about losing her job in an ambush meeting?

If HR works against employees who are not on the management team, as every single one of these posts indicate, then companies need to start making that clear instead of hiding behind the dangerous lie that HR is there to help resolve employee issues. Either get rid of these departments altogether or give them a more appropriate name like 'Management Protection' because they are obviously making it their job to evade the employment laws to protect managers and executives. The mission of many of these departments has morphed into something very malevolent. Whether it is fear of lawsuits or fear of fighting corruption within the companies themselves, many of these departments no longer uphold current laws but rather skirt the law to protect incompetent and harassing managers and punish whistle blowers. The majority of American workers are ignorant of this little known fact and unsuspectingly walk into a lion's den when they go to HR with complaints and concerns.

My advice to this particular woman would be to go out and buy a flash drive and save every single file on her hard drive, along with any email communications between her and the supervisor in question. Also, if she has time, write down every statement she remembers her co-workers making about the hostile environment they are in because she can pretty much conclude that the reason her colleagues were not invited to the meeting is because they have already expressed to the director that they do not feel the environment is hostile. Assume you are now out there on your own and be ready to have the tables turned on you by making you the problem; not the supervisor. Prepare your mind for hearing some pretty outrageous accusations made against you. Get ready to hear statements you made get repeated in a way that is totally out of context but which supports the narrative they are consciously creating that makes you out to be the one creating hostility within the department. Be prepared for a warning at best and termination of your employment at worst. Regardless, know that your continued employment within the supervisor's department is over and your continued existence at the company is tenable. With a director and supervisor against you, it will not be long before they line up HR against you, if they have not already done so. Expect that your personnel file has been tampered with and any future evaluations will not be favorable so that they can continue to support their narrative of you as the trouble-maker.

Record the meeting and if your state is a state that requires two-party notice for recording, record it anyway because as new facts come to light, they <u>will</u> deny what they said. At least you will have them on tape and it will be something your attorney can use if you decide to pursue a lawsuit.

I realize my advice is not what any employee who loves her job wants to hear. Obviously, this employee is engaged in her job and the company or she would not have come forward with her concerns. My heart bleeds for her because I can see the writing on the wall just as all the people who posted comments saw it. She is in a losing position if her goal is to remain in her current job and career and the sooner she realizes it the better the outcome will be in terms of her survival. She should place herself first from this moment forward. Update her resume. Remain grounded in the truth and when the supervisor and director begin turning the tables on her, repeat the truth without any emotion whatsoever. As they distort her statements and say her colleagues have no problem with the supervisor, then she should realize immediately that her colleagues are not the friends she thought they were. She should refer to the sheet she prepared before the meeting regarding what she remembers them saying and bring in any email communications that support her contentions. She is not being traitorous. She is being truthful unlike them. She may not win the battle of keeping her job but she will leave that room with her head held high and her integrity intact. She will not believe the confidence and strength that will give her in her journey toward her ultimate destiny. She will go forward knowing that she was in the wrong company working for the wrong people and she did not conform her integrity in order to become like them. Although it may not feel like it in the moment, she will have won the war. When she returns to an environment of rationality where people say what they mean and mean what they say, she will be able to feel sorry for all the losers who compromised their souls to the craziness around them for the small price of a paycheck.

Bullying And Mobbing Is A Safety Issue

Abuse of power like bullying and mobbing cause psychological injury and just as emphasis and training is put on preventing physical injury in the workplace, the same due diligence should be applied to preventing injury from abusive management practices. Safety was this corporation's mantra. They always spoke about the safety of its employees being tantamount. Physical safety, of course, is extremely important and should be emphasized, but along with it should be concern for a person's psychological safety. The company had a safety policy which allowed any employee to stop production at any time if they perceived a safety hazard. Production would not resume until the safety issue was resolved. The same kind of policy should be in place in cases of bullying. If the company suspects that one of its employees is being bullied, a full investigation should take place and a resolution reached that satisfies all parties. If the employee continues to work with the power abuser, the work relationship should be monitored over a period of time to ensure that the abuse of power stops completely. If the investigation and follow-up is handled properly and fairly, there is no reason why a resolution satisfactory to both parties cannot be reached. Under no circumstances should the bullying ever be allowed to escalate to the point where a mobbing occurs and psychological injury to the victim is thereby a certainty.

Two-Way Communication is Meaningless Without Truth

We (the communications department) should have partnered more with career and development in management training. Face-to-face communication is worthless if people do not know how to speak honestly and forthrightly without condemning. But it takes more than communication. The right people need to be chosen in the first place. A manager should be self aware and not be afraid of the facing the truth in himself or the people he is leading. When the going got tough, Kristine was unable to assume her role as a leader. She was not mentally equipped to be a director of the corporation. She lied to me and was going to fire me based on allegations she knew were false. Those are the actions of a cowardly, little girl who wants to please, not those of a manager whose role it is to help their team members solve their problems. She kept sending me back into a toxic mess to deal with it myself, knowing that I did not have the power to do anything about it on my own.

When Kristine told me in one of my evaluations that I wasn't the kind of leader the company looks for, she prefaced it with the phrase, "I want to be transparent." Transparency is vital in all human interactions. But what exactly does that term mean? To me, it means not hiding what you think or feel. Kristine was being clear in telling me what she thought about my potential, but was she in a position to make that value judgment when she herself was such a deficient leader?

A manager who is deficient in character and skills will never be able to properly coach and lead his team. If organizations promote people who do not possess the requisite character or skills required for managing people, then they are placing their employees in a perilous situation. I think we underestimate the power a manager holds and we promote people all the time who are not prepared to assume the responsibilities of managing (or appoint them in the case of organizations under authoritarian rule). They do not know how to get the best out of the people in their care and they cave into pressure, even if it means harming another employee. I use the term "care" purposefully. A manager's team members are in his care, not under his control. This is the whole idea of servant leadership and what Jesus tried to show his disciples by washing their feet at the last supper. No one is better than anyone else. The role of managers is to use the tools at their disposal to make the organization profitable. It is incumbent on them to get to know each of their team members individually and find out what makes them tick. What are their goals? Why are they working for this particular company? What gets them excited about coming to work each day? Is there anything they dread about coming to work? First, however, they need to ask these questions of themselves. If a manager is not willing to confront his own weaknesses, then he renders himself incapable of improving. If one is unable to improve and grow through self-awareness, they will inevitably encounter situations that are beyond their ability to handle. They will naturally blame others for their own inadequacies because in a mind that never seeks to learn about its own inadequacies, there are no perceived inadequacies. The blame will naturally fall on someone else's shoulders.

This was where Rick was. His large ego fooled him into thinking that admitting his unease with change would tar his image as the team leader of the change management team. He certainly couldn't tell his executive buddies about his insecurities and probably not even his wife who viewed him as the capable vice president of a global corporation. The only one he felt comfortable enough to speak to honestly was his victim of abuse. I later realized that at the time he was confiding in me, he and his consultant partner were instituting their strategy of isolation and non-work to get rid of me. This man has taken evil to the next level. He would have been quite comfortable in a Nazi uniform toying with the emotions and mental health of his Jewish victims. I was a safe haven for this man to express his consciousness of truth. If he told anyone else the whole house of cards he was building his career and life on could come crashing down.

When I wrote the letter to HR, I think he viewed it as a direct attack against him. His fear of being exposed caused him to begin his behind-the-scenes campaign to paint me as an incompetent troublemaker. When I reviewed the letter a couple of years later after undergoing my own self-examination, I realized that I may have read it the same way if I were him. I kept denying it, but maybe it was a direct, frontal attack against him since I wrote it right after his condescending email and I was angry at the way he was treating me and my work. Although my opinion of him as a manipulative coward has not changed, I definitely could have been more diplomatic in the letter while still achieving my goal to be truthful in how I viewed what was going on.

A very important aspect in a target's fight for survival is understanding the enemy. In a sense, I did what I hated Rick for doing to me. I attacked him at his core. His ego was extremely fragile because he was in a situation he felt uncomfortable in but was compensating for with his authoritarian style of leadership. He hated me as much as he eventually made me hate him and he fed his hate with revenge. I fed mine in an alternate way. Hate, insecurity, fear, naivety and ignorance fed the beast of the bullying and mobbing. Although we both lost the battle by succumbing to hate, we both won our individual wars in the end. I do not want to get too deep or spiritual, but we both got what we wanted out of a horrible experience and although I am glad it happened in the sense that it woke me up to the reality of human nature, I sure as hell wish I had been given this information as a child so that I would have been better equipped to fight the battles and deal more constructively with the aftermath.

6
The Power Of One (Individual)

A Question Every Whistle Blower Asks: Would I Do It Again?

I read that Ed has moved on to an equally powerful and lucrative position at another company and my manager heads up the human resources department for a different global corporation. The powerful and well-connected always get recycled don't they? It seems like they are never made to pay for their misdeeds. It is bad enough that they are never punished. In most cases they are rewarded. The politician caught in a scandal goes away for a few years and comes back as a consultant on a cable news network. The bullying boss who is denied a congressional post becomes the go-to expert on fighting terrorism. The businessman convicted of fraud becomes a best selling author after doing his stint. The perception is that the rich and powerful are immune from the [in]justice doled out to the rest of us. After awhile, it becomes a part of the human psyche. People become afraid to speak up because they don't want to put themselves on the line knowing nothing will get done if they do.

Why didn't anyone help me? I was in a couple of protected classes. Why are so many victims of bullying and mobbing left on their own? Why are Ed, Kristine and others like them able to move into positions of equivalent power and prestige, while their victims are left struggling to stay afloat emotionally, mentally and financially? Could it be that they are able to use their powerful contacts as references to "move on" to other positions, while they make it impossible for their victims to move on with their lives after having set out to purposefully and maliciously destroy their personal and professional reputations?

Our laws fail us when power can trump those laws. Few, if any of us, have the consciousness of a man like Jesus who can see beyond the shortcomings of our tormentors to ask God to forgive them for their ignorance. It is therefore ironic that we have put ourselves in the position of having to acquire that level of consciousness if we want any sense of joy and peace in a mindless physical world that is becoming more evil and less free by the day. More cases like mine are bound to occur simply because they can. We have placed our consciousness of right and wrong in the hands of the wealthy and powerful and have thereby condemned ourselves to living by their authority if we want to retain a paycheck.

We can continue passing laws to address our problems but what good are laws when we have people like the attorney in this company who can choose not to follow them when it serves their own personal interests not to? Ed Odom took an oath to uphold the law when he became an attorney, yet he did not uphold it with regard to me. He avoided it and in his avoidance of it, my life as I had constructed it up to that point was completely destroyed. Yet passing laws continues to be our answer to everything. Just read the news. If there is a problem, then there is an outcry to pass a law to address it. There is little if any talk of the underlying factors that cause these problems to exist in the first place. Ever since this mobbing took place against me, whenever I read a story about workplace shootings I see all the same patterns that everyone else fails to see because I lived through them and am here to write about them. Fortunately for me, I am not dead or in some prison cell wondering why it is me in there and not the ruthless gang whose actions drove a rational and creative individual to commit such an irrational and destructive act.

There was no solution for me because the corruption, resignation and defeat had seeped into every crevice of this company. Management and HR set the standards below what any decent human being would consider acceptable behavior and all the others just followed in line like mindless automatons. How many other complaints did Ed handle with such a blatant disregard of the rule of law and standards of ethical behavior? How many other people did he and other managers like Kristine refer to psychologists and then fire so that their voices were silenced? And now Ed smiles back at me from the pages of the Internet announcing his arrival at a company that has no idea about the human hazard to which it has exposed its employees.

I have had to ask myself, if faced with the situation again, whether or not I would write the original, whistle-blowing letter to HR about the mismanagement of the project. Although that letter was not the trigger for the mobbing, I now know it sealed my fate. My job was lost as soon as I hit the send button on my computer. My two teammates had voiced similar concerns, but in the words of my former manager "they did it the smart way" by keeping silent and getting rewarded with jobs outside the project and away from the bully VP and consultant. Although they were not managers, they both maintained close relationships with managers who showed them the ropes. They knew the real rules of the company and they decided to protect themselves.

Given these facts, I have struggled with answering for myself the question of whether or not I would ever have written the letter if I had it to do over again knowing what I know now. What I have concluded is that asking this question of myself is totally pointless. We live in a world where we can only know the past and the present. The future remains to be written. When I look at the experience now it is through the consciousness of a different person than the one I was then. Your own consciousness is different from mine. We all act based on the state of our own minds at any given moment. For myself, I think the experience was a blessing in disguise. One of my last emails to the HR manager during that weekend when I called the ethics officer said, "I will never give credit to any person or organization who does not deserve it."

I was a propagandist acting in ignorance and every communication I wrote was a lie. My words put people in danger of finding themselves in the same situation that caused me so much pain and misery. The mobbing woke me up to the truth in the only way most of us wake up: through personal experience. We can read books like this one, go to school and listen to the advice of other people but it is the nature of the human mind to learn through personal experience. It was all so damned difficult but I am so damned grateful for being made aware of who I really am and what I really want from my life. I never want to act in ignorance again. I want to remain conscious and aware so that I have the grace, wisdom and courage to conduct my life right. The past is the past. I need to learn from it and grow in the direction of where I want my life force to go.

Lawsuits

Our criminal justice system puts the emphasis on negative reinforcement in the form of punishment. Very little focus is given to prevention by way of creating a population of people who find it not only wrong to hurt another human being, but illogical in the sense that they are defeating their purpose for being on this earth.

Making the choice not to pursue punishment in the form of a lawsuit allowed all the perpetrators of the mobbing to continue on unimpeded in their careers with no punishment for their actions. They all walked away scot-free and I think about that a lot. I know the law tells me they work for the company and the company is liable for their actions but even if I had been mentally and psychologically up to suing the company, I don't think any monetary outcome would have satisfied my desire for justice. I blame them all personally for the damage they did to me and my family. Initiating a lawsuit would not have let my father know that his daughter is not a failure. It would not have put me back on the same personal and professional trajectory I was on. It would not have given me back the mental and physical health they took from me. It would not have given me back any of the life they unjustly stole from me. It may have just given me a little bit more money, but even that is doubtful. I was in an extremely vulnerable and weakened mental and emotional condition after they were through with me. I believe facing what they were doing and saying about me when I was not ready very likely would have bolstered their allegations that I was mentally unstable. It would have been unbearable.

The law didn't stop them from doing what they did and it wouldn't have helped me retrieve what I most desired. I don't think most lawsuits even send a message anymore. These people were all prepared for a lawsuit. They did what they wanted to do anyway. They didn't care. If I sued, the money wouldn't have come out of their pockets. They would have destroyed what little they left of my reputation in defending themselves and I would still have had to fight the uphill battle for my emotional, mental and physical well being, only it would have taken much longer and been way more agonizing because they would have made sure it. All this because I questioned the manner in which a project was getting managed.

For well over two years, I carried so much guilt over not suing them because as it stands now, that is the only remedy provided to victims. They had no right to take my economic livelihood away from me. No person deserves that fate for stating their opinion. A lawsuit would have been the only way to get these people to understand that what they did is wrong. Or would it? They were all expecting the lawsuit. Lawsuits have become a cost of doing business. Companies factor them in along with all the other costs of business. The perpetrators knew this which is why they chose the sadistic strategy of mobbing to get rid of me. A lawsuit wouldn't have punished any of them and it would have completely destroyed me. The courts favor employers and they had already gotten their ducks in a row to decimate me in court. I wouldn't even have had the truth because I do not believe I could have recovered from the PTSD, depression and total lack of focus while a lawsuit was going on.

I find comfort in believing that they all spent many nights worrying about the lawsuit that never came knowing they were all guilty as hell. By walking out on my job, it left them with the threat of a constructive discharge looming over their heads. Although they probably doubled up their efforts to bolster their mental instability claims, I instilled in them the fear of the unknown. I never told my teammate I wasn't suing, so the control was back in my hands even though I was not consciously aware of it. I can imagine that they had many secretive, closed door meetings where instead of plotting how to get rid of me, they were plotting their next moves to protect themselves. All for nothing. Who knows. Maybe by unknowingly using their own strategy against them – by not acknowledging them with a lawsuit – I made them suffer more. It could have been like a science fiction book I once read where the aliens hovering above the earth ignored the atomic bomb that was detonated but failed to destroy its ship. They didn't retaliate or even acknowledge they knew a bomb had gone off. The people in government who activated the bomb destroyed themselves with recriminations. Is that part of turning the other cheek? Be smarter and use their own methods against them?

Having faith in your own strategy to always follow a positive and truthful path takes you beyond the need for lawsuits. I will be fine no matter what I experience in this world because I am not living for the external rewards that have been created for our illusory egoistic structures. That is what all the people who tortured me were living for and I have no desire to ever be like them. I don't ever want to make anyone go through what I did if that is part of my job description. There is no amount of money that would be worth the pain they put me through.

Lawsuits

Our criminal justice system puts the emphasis on negative reinforcement in the form of punishment. Very little focus is given to prevention by way of creating a population of people who find it not only wrong to hurt another human being, but illogical in the sense that they are defeating their purpose for being on this earth.

Making the choice not to pursue punishment in the form of a lawsuit allowed all the perpetrators of the mobbing to continue on unimpeded in their careers with no punishment for their actions. They all walked away scot-free and I think about that a lot. I know the law tells me they work for the company and the company is liable for their actions but even if I had been mentally and psychologically up to suing the company, I don't think any monetary outcome would have satisfied my desire for justice. I blame them all personally for the damage they did to me and my family. Initiating a lawsuit would not have let my father know that his daughter is not a failure. It would not have put me back on the same personal and professional trajectory I was on. It would not have given me back the mental and physical health they took from me. It would not have given me back any of the life they unjustly stole from me. It may have just given me a little bit more money, but even that is doubtful. I was in an extremely vulnerable and weakened mental and emotional condition after they were through with me. I believe facing what they were doing and saying about me when I was not ready very likely would have bolstered their allegations that I was mentally unstable. It would have been unbearable.

The law didn't stop them from doing what they did and it wouldn't have helped me retrieve what I most desired. I don't think most lawsuits even send a message anymore. These people were all prepared for a lawsuit. They did what they wanted to do anyway. They didn't care. If I sued, the money wouldn't have come out of their pockets. They would have destroyed what little they left of my reputation in defending themselves and I would still have had to fight the uphill battle for my emotional, mental and physical well being, only it would have taken much longer and been way more agonizing because they would have made sure it. All this because I questioned the manner in which a project was getting managed.

For well over two years, I carried so much guilt over not suing them because as it stands now, that is the only remedy provided to victims. They had no right to take my economic livelihood away from me. No person deserves that fate for stating their opinion. A lawsuit would have been the only way to get these people to understand that what they did is wrong. Or would it? They were all expecting the lawsuit. Lawsuits have become a cost of doing business. Companies factor them in along with all the other costs of business. The perpetrators knew this which is why they chose the sadistic strategy of mobbing to get rid of me. A lawsuit wouldn't have punished any of them and it would have completely destroyed me. The courts favor employers and they had already gotten their ducks in a row to decimate me in court. I wouldn't even have had the truth because I do not believe I could have recovered from the PTSD, depression and total lack of focus while a lawsuit was going on.

I find comfort in believing that they all spent many nights worrying about the lawsuit that never came knowing they were all guilty as hell. By walking out on my job, it left them with the threat of a constructive discharge looming over their heads. Although they probably doubled up their efforts to bolster their mental instability claims, I instilled in them the fear of the unknown. I never told my teammate I wasn't suing, so the control was back in my hands even though I was not consciously aware of it. I can imagine that they had many secretive, closed door meetings where instead of plotting how to get rid of me, they were plotting their next moves to protect themselves. All for nothing. Who knows. Maybe by unknowingly using their own strategy against them – by not acknowledging them with a lawsuit – I made them suffer more. It could have been like a science fiction book I once read where the aliens hovering above the earth ignored the atomic bomb that was detonated but failed to destroy its ship. They didn't retaliate or even acknowledge they knew a bomb had gone off. The people in government who activated the bomb destroyed themselves with recriminations. Is that part of turning the other cheek? Be smarter and use their own methods against them?

Having faith in your own strategy to always follow a positive and truthful path takes you beyond the need for lawsuits. I will be fine no matter what I experience in this world because I am not living for the external rewards that have been created for our illusory egoistic structures. That is what all the people who tortured me were living for and I have no desire to ever be like them. I don't ever want to make anyone go through what I did if that is part of my job description. There is no amount of money that would be worth the pain they put me through.

The Buck Stops With Each of Us

It almost feels like I have come full circle. Here I am giving advice about how I think companies should be managed and that is what the power abusers at the company I worked for hung their hats on the first time I tried giving management advice in my letter to HR. I guess I can't help myself. If I get criticized this time around, so be it. All I know is that something is very wrong with the state of organizational management and it is negatively affecting so many people without the power to do anything about it. With an estimated one out of six employees in America currently being bullied and a majority of the workforce acting as bystanders cowering in fear and unwilling to help, I will never allow myself to be silenced again. I will speak out against this scourge with all the strength of my being and in whatever forum I am blessed to be given.

I believe I have been as hard on myself in this book as I have been on Rick, Stephanie and the other work colleagues who mobbed me. However, I do not want to give the impression to other victims of this workplace abuse that they are in any way at fault or in any way brought the treatment on themselves. They are not and did not. The blame lies solely with the power abusers and their enablers who have not learned how to live with their fellow men and women in a civilized society and the organizations who allow and condone this behavior by anyone in their workforce.

The problem of bullying will continue unabated unless we address the flaws in our human character by getting to the root of what ails us. The corrupt and powerful will gain in strength because they are simply following their nature to exert power to retain their power. The weaker and less powerful need to begin following their true natures of spirit within. The power that Marcus, Ed and Rick possessed was illusory. It was fueled by their titles and their ability to instill fear in the hearts of the employees who were beneath them. As long as we sheepishly hand over our individual divinity to them and others like them, there is no reason to think that any of us will be able to escape the fate of becoming a target ourselves at some point in our lives.

I have never gotten an apology from any of them and probably never will. In the few conversations I had with my teammate and the HR manager when I was still unaware of their complicity, it was clear they had convinced themselves that they were just doing their jobs. Theirs was not to question the authority of the man in the executive suite or think on their own. Theirs was to curry favor by doing what they were told to do and accept a pay check and any favors they could garner in return. This is how they perceived the game is played in America. One of them told me as much when new leadership took over. She said she was looking for a job at an American company because this one didn't understand that it is money that motivates the American worker. Any company that tries to instill a sense of pride in what it is producing is a cult in her eyes. This is what the American dream has been reduced to after years of exalting greed and crony capitalism on Wall Street, in Washington D.C and in board rooms across the country. And it is reflected in survey after survey. A 2013 Gallup poll which examined worker engagement from 2010 to 2012 showed that seven out of 10 workers have "checked out" at work or are "actively disengaged."

The results of this new way of thinking were on full display with these executives' handling of me and my concerns. I was a low paid, low level, ignorant employee without a voice. What nerve I must have displayed in their eyes when I dared to question one of their own. The good news is that bullying and mobbing are learned behaviors and any behavior that is learned can be unlearned when people no longer see any benefit in it. On a school level, the case needs to be made that great minds are being stunted and promising students are dropping out of school, or worse - committing suicide, as a result of bullying. On the corporate level, it must be understood that corporations are entities with a profit motive, so the case needs to be made persuasively that these kinds of management practices are unprofitable in terms of lost productivity, time, money, innovation, company resources and human capital.

Conclusion

I had the good sense to walk out of the company after the Ethics Officer creepily asked me what the psychiatrist I never saw said, instead of responsibly investigating what I told him. However, I was unable to escape the debilitating physical and mental symptoms that result from severe negative stress. My own recovery was very spiritual in nature. I could not have gotten through each day without the comfort of knowing that there is a force without and within me that is working for my good. The path I took to heal my wounded mind took me to many self-help books and spiritual texts, including the Bible. What I discovered in reading the Bible for the first time in my life is that it is filled with stories of bullying, mobbing and trauma, on both a personal and societal level. What I learned from these stories is that no one, abuser and abused alike, comes away from the experience unscathed. I would like to end this book with one of these stories.

King David's son, Absalom, had a beautiful sister named Tamar who David's other son, Amnon, loved. He was in such anguish over his sister Tamar that he became sick. She was a virgin and Amnon thought it impossible to do anything to her. Amnon had a friend named Jonadab, son of David's brother Shimeah, who was very clever. When Amnon told him how he loved Tamar but that she was his sister and there was nothing he could do, Jonadab gave him a strategy for getting her into his bed. He told him to pretend to be sick so that when the King visited him, he could request that the king send Tamar to him to encourage him to eat.

His plan worked perfectly. After visiting Amnon, King David told Tamar to prepare some food for Amnon. Tamar does as she is told and prepares some cakes for him to eat. When she arrives at his house, Amnon has everyone leave his room so that Tamar can feed him. Unsuspecting of his motives, Tamar brings the cakes she prepared into the bedroom. When she brings them to him, he tells her, "Come! Lie with me, my sister!" But she answers him, "No my brother! Do not force me! Do not commit this terrible crime. Where would I take my shame? And you will be labeled a fool in Israel. So please, speak to the King; he will not keep me from you. But Amnon would not listen to her. He was too strong for her; he forced her down and raped her. Then Amnon felt intense hatred for her; the hatred he felt for her far surpassed the love he previously had for her. Amnon said to her, "Get up, leave." She replied, "No, brother, because sending me away would be far worse than this evil thing you have done to me." He would not listen to her, but called the youth who was his attendant and said, "Send this girl outside, away from me, and bar the door after her." Now she had on a long tunic, for that is how virgin princesses dressed in olden days. When his attendant put her out and barred the door after her, Tamar put ashes on her head and tore the long tunic in which she was clothed. Then, putting her hands to her head she went away crying loudly. Her brother Absalom said to her: "Has your brother Amnon been with you? Keep still now, my sister, he is your brother. Do not take this so to heart." [In other words, just shut up and take it] So Tamar remained devastated in the house of her brother Absalom.

When King David heard of the whole affair, he became very angry. He would not, however, antagonize Amnon, his high-spirited son. He loved him because he was his firstborn. And like the good enabler and bystander he was, Absalom said nothing to Amnon. All the same, he hated Amnon for what he did to Tamar and two years later, Absalom killed Amnon. The Bible says King David wept bitterly at the news. Absalom fled and stayed Geshur for three years, during which David mourned.

Amnon hated Tamar after he raped her. This is the psychology of a corrupted mind. Blame and hate the victim. People keep asking how an atrocity like the holocaust could have happened. It was because the Jews in Nazi Germany were hated. For a long time after the mobbing, I kept thinking my manager cared about me and I had no idea about the deception of my teammates and colleagues. Never in my wildest dreams would I have thought they hated me. What I have since learned is that the victims of crime and abuse are always hated and have to be hated in order for the perpetrators to justify their actions in their own minds. Tamar's pleas for Amnon to act righteously after the rape fell on deaf ears because it was not his nature to act righteously. If he was a righteous man, he would never have raped her. It was like me trying to get the ethics officer to act ethically and investigate what I told him. If he was an ethical man, he never would have engaged in the mobbing.

When I sent the email to the teammate who betrayed me telling her I figured out what they did, she asked me what it was that I needed. I needed someone to say they were sorry. Like Tamar, I needed someone to say that what was done was wrong - that they put me in an unsafe environment and they were sorry for that. Just like the "move on" email I received from the HR vice president, Tamar was told by Absalom to get over it and everything was swept under the rug because David loved Amnon and didn't want him to have to pay for what he did. No one was held accountable and the victim of the attack was the only one made to suffer.

I do not know what will happen to the perpetrators of the mobbing over the course of their lives but I do know that energy is eternal. The negative energy they used to perpetrate the mobbing and then cover it up after I was gone is out there and will be neutralized at some point. Absalom was never able to forget what Amnon did and Amnon eventually paid with his life. David suffered the pain of losing a son and Absalom was banished from his home while David mourned. All because each of them were unwilling to handle the situation justly in the immediate aftermath of the crime. If Amnon had been made to pay for his crime, Absalom would have been happy and would not have taken revenge. Tamar would have been vindicated and would have been able to live her life with pride instead of shame. David would have proved he was a just king who treated all people fairly, even when his own family was responsible. All parties would have received the justice and peace they deserve if the situation had just been handled ethically and fairly to begin with.

I do not care how many laws are passed, bullying and mobbing behavior will never end until the perpetrators are the ones made to feel ashamed - not their victims. It is time to take the responsibility upon ourselves to learn the tactics and rationalizations used by bullies and mobs in our families, schools, workplaces and governments so that we can recognize them when they are used and punish the proper parties. Not one more victim of an abuse of power should be punished for having done nothing wrong – particularly since the Bible made us aware of the tactics used by power abusers centuries ago.

People pay a price for their sins at some point. Even the powerful pay and sometimes they pay in a far worse way than if they had just handled the mess they made at the time it happened. It takes courage to do the right thing when we know our own self interests will be negatively impacted by doing so. Our natural urge is to protect ourselves and the ones we love. As hard as it is to admit, self-protection was at the root of all the corruption that consumed the workplace I was in. The CEO knew his appointed vice presidents would protect him. The vice presidents knew they would be protected by the managers and directors and the managers and directors knew they were safe as long as they followed their marching orders. The employees who stayed quiet and did as they were told were protected as well. The corporation spouted a message all day long about transparency, communication and the need for change but the reality was that it was at a standstill because change was something the CEO could not handle. Change would put him in unfamiliar territory and outside of the knowledge base he obtained from the previous CEO who taught him the ropes. His self image was threatened with every message he gave if his message was internalized by the employees under him. He was a very dangerous character who should never have been given the reigns of leadership. Although I blame my manager and ethics officer the most, the reality is that they were appointed to their positions by this cowardly man and knew if they wanted to keep their positions and their work references intact, then they better follow his commands.

I was one of the employees who internalized the messages the CEO gave. Like trickle down economics, corruption flows downward and I was caught downwind in the shit storm my letter to HR generated when the truth it told directly affected the self interests of all the leaders involved in the project. My own knowledge base about basic human nature was lacking and it was my undoing. I hope this book has served to expand the knowledge base of you, the reader, so that when you find yourself downwind in a corrupt environment you have the necessary mental tools to escape the kind of confusion, hopelessness, shame and guilt that Tamar and I both undeservedly took upon ourselves in our ignorance.

The Old Testament verses found in Sirach 18:19-20 say, "Before you speak, learn. Before you get sick, prepare the cure. Before you are judged, examine yourself, and at the time of scrutiny, you will have forgiveness." I want you, the reader, to learn before you speak and have the cure before you get sick. I want you to have the self awareness to protect yourself and others if you ever find yourself in a war for your own mental, emotional, physical and/or financial survival. No matter what you do, do it consciously. As these verses tell us, you cannot prepare the cure after getting the sickness. You have to prepare it ahead of time. You can learn to live by your wits (listen to your intuition) but for now, you must learn basic skills. It is my heartfelt hope that this book strengthens your skill set and provides you with some useful information in coming up with a successful strategy if you ever find yourself targeted by powerful self interests. Your greatest strength will be their greatest weakness because they count on you being mentally unprepared for the assault.

Surprise is always the enemy. Use your knowledge to turn the tables on them and surprise them at every turn. You deserve the win – not the shame and guilt they want to lay at your feet for doing the right thing. Fling that shit back at them and let them slip and slide in it like the swine they are. You will walk away with your integrity intact knowing you did not wait around for someone else to prepare the cure for you like Tamar and I did. You prepared it yourself ahead of time and now that you have it, you will never, ever be sick again.

The End

Choose Your Battles Wisely

A man came to my house last week,
saying the government would like a peek -
inside the workings of my home and mind
threatening fines if I was to decline.

He asked me what I drive to work.
Is my emotional health a cause for concern?
How well do I hear, can I climb the stairs -
am I disabled, blind or receiving welfare?

Thirty pages later I was somewhat numb.
Had I just turned my life over to someone so dumb?
I felt shame at giving in to all his quisling tactics
by providing him access to my daily practices,

My line was to be drawn when they came to my home -
that would be the time I'd enter this war.
It was so easy making choice an either/or
before it came knocking on my own front door.

APPENDIX

Letter to the HR Manager

I have written and revised this letter over and over again trying to parse my words and finesse the language in a way so that no one gets offended and my own position in the grand scheme of things is somehow secured. I have come to realize, however, that such an approach is not my style, has never worked for me and will not work for me in this situation. As you know from our talk, I feel passionately about how I see things progressing on this project and I can settle for no less than to state my opinion and let the cards fall where they may.

I have been on the project since the middle of April. I cannot tell you how proud I was to be asked to be on this project and how equally proud my entire family was for me. I was actually in a state disbelief for a couple of days or so after Kristine talked to me about it. However, it didn't take long for the shock to turn into an overwhelming sense of excitement at the prospect of being part of a global project that would transform the way our company does business for the foreseeable future.

From a more personal standpoint, I felt like this was the opportunity I had been working towards my entire career. All the late nights, hard work and studying had led me to this and I was finally going to be able to take the lead in a field I absolutely love and am really good at.

I thought the team working environment would be a dynamic, collaborative and learning environment where we would be brainstorming strategies with a group of equally talented and motivated people who were great at what they do. Together, we would work as a team to find the best approach for successfully implementing the business system throughout the North American organization.

In my previous role in Internal Communications, I had the opportunity to work with many of the people on this team and I really do believe the company chose the best and the brightest minds for the project. Unfortunately, I have also come to believe that the brain trust that was put together to ensure success for the project is being squandered due to a lack of strong leadership on the North American team.

This is my own conclusion, of course. Although I have a good feeling about how other people on the project feel, I cannot speak for them. I can only express what I feel from my own perspective and hope that I am able to convey my opinions in a constructive manner that does not denigrate anyone on the team.

1. The Change Management process is being run by the consulting firm, not the project team.

From where I sit, the consultants are running the show. I would like to say up front that I have never worked with consultants before and this may be how it is done on projects like this. But in my view, it's not working. The North American team leadership works directly with the consultants and seeks little, if any input, from the team. I overhear conversations that Rick and Mike have with the two consultants about communications, change impact and other strategies, but I have never been asked to participate in any of these meetings and, as far as I can tell, the other members of the team have never been included either. It is like one team member said to me, "We are like a façade. We're here to look like we are being used, but it's all for show."

It is like a one size fits all approach. All our communications are being prepared from Power Point decks that the consultants prepare. I have gone to Rick twice and exasperatingly asked him what my role and function here is, and have not gotten a really good answer because I don't think he knows. Roles and responsibilities have never been spelled out.

2. Inadequate planning.

Even now, the only project plan we have is the project timeline that was prepared in the beginning of the project. In a recent lunch meeting, one of the team members brought up the fact that they had a week of down-time after the first validation, in which everyone had nothing to do. He wanted to know what the plan was after the second validation takes place in July, when the configuration phase begins. The answer was that that might be a good time for people to take their vacations. As far as I can tell from the original project timeline, configuration is expected to take six months to complete!

I am certainly not a project manager, but it seems to me that they could be using this time to meet, brainstorm and come up with an action plan for this project that details out the actions to be taken from here on out. Instead, the few tasks (and I do mean tasks) are given out in drip form, with no independent thought as to overall strategy. We are literally sitting here for huge blocks of time with nothing to do.

3. Lack of Creativity

In a lunch meeting with Gary Boire, he said we will need to sell this to the company. I spent a lot of time thinking about that and the message and approach we should take to communicate the system to the people who will be using it. I talked to my counterpart overseas about my thoughts and ideas and she thought they were great. Together, we were going to work on a plan to implement them. When I sent our initial ideas (along with a Power Point presentation that laid out the message in simple terms ... no hard-to-follow diagrams and language), the email I got back was that they had decided on a strategy that was put together by Stephanie.

I also asked Rick if any members of the team would be attending the road shows to the locations to present the strategy to the change agents and he said that he would be handling alone. That's fine. They can use whatever approach they like ... it's their call. My problem is that this, and all the other decisions on this project, are being made without any discussion or input whatsoever from us ... the employees who were chosen for our expertise and knowledge.

I don't know much, but I do know this company. I know its values because I am literally a living, breathing example of them. This company has allowed me to fulfill my potential in more ways than I can say and given me the chance to utilize all the talents and abilities God has given me. I try to channel a piece of that passion in every article I write and every campaign I conduct for this company. And I know that everyone on this team can say they approach their careers and positions in the same way.

Can an outside consultant say that?

I have applied to a Masters program in Education. Hopefully I will be accepted and start in the fall. It would be so easy to sit here doing the tasks that are assigned to me like setting up luncheons, filling out calendars with dates and transcribing minutes. I could work nine to five and sneak in a homework assignment or two when I am sitting here with nothing to do.

However, that is not how I function and when I boil it down to its simplest terms, it is not what I signed up for. I feel unmotivated, disengaged and underutilized. Those feelings are corrosive to the project and to the team and if even one other person feels the way I do, it does not bode well for success.

I have been told that things will get better once the roll-out begins in North America. That might be true and it might not. I don't know because no plan or strategy has been presented to us. I am not a manager and would not presume to tell a manager or leader how to lead his team. There are as many varieties of managing and leading as there are leaders themselves. Having said that, I do know from my own personal experience that some styles work and some styles don't. It is my belief that the top-down, consultant heavy style being used to lead this project is not working.

Given the magnitude and scope of this project, I would just ask that someone review and analyze the situation to see if this is the best approach, or if there are alternative methods of working that will make this environment more team-oriented and make our people more productive.

Thanks for listening.

Feedback On Communications for the North American Team

I. More structured and consistent communications

In all the meetings I had, the main take-away was that there has to be more structure and consistency in the communication and messaging, both within the NA team and in the communications between NA and the teams overseas. Some of the points brought up were:

> ¬ There needs to be more structure in the way information is communicated. They are happening upon much of it by chance. An example was cited that some changes were made to the ██, but none of the coordinators were notified of the changes.

> ¬ Next steps need to be clearly defined. The teams don't really know what to do next.

> ¬ Need to know the next steps for integration. They need to be given a consistent approach for identifying touch points and provided with a strategy for how they will be handled. If they do not have a consistent approach, they will just end up looking at ██ to try to identify them.

> ¬ The consulting company could be giving more direction than they are. They feel like there must be best practices / templates they use. They need to share them. They don't know if the strategy is to not provide this information, so they will come up with the processes on their own. But, whatever the strategy, it needs to be shared with the team.

II. Team Activities

Everyone I spoke to liked the idea of having activities where all the team members can get together and talk. They thought the pizza luncheon was good. Some other ideas were:

> ¬ Lunch 'n Learns

These should be in-person, not Live Meeting, and should not last more than one-hour. They all voiced that they would like to use these meetings to learn more about the details of SAP, such as

- How to place an order in the new system
- How to create a requisition

Also, it would be nice if pizza or sandwiches were served.

¬ Something after work like a Happy Hour, bowling, Gameworks, baseball game

¬ Pot-Luck Luncheon

III. Celebration / Recognition

They all liked the idea of getting everyone together for a monthly birthday celebration, with cake. As far as recognition, one team member said he would like the recognition to point out what the person did well, so that others can learn from it and use as a best practice.

Possible Action Items:

¬ Work with Stephanie to determine topics/speakers for Lunch 'n Learns and send schedule out to team members

¬ Given that the team members are mainly interested in information they can use to move forward, I would reconsider the idea of a team newsletter.

One person suggested having Mike send out a regular message (weekly, bi-weekly), where he shares information like:

o Strategy
o High-level updates
o Where we are in the project
o Where we are headed
o Goals and objectives for the coming week
o Next steps
o Milestones.

¬ Then we could use communication boards for communicating team news like birthdays, month-at-a-glance, member profiles, milestones, stories to share, photos, celebrations, recognitions, etc.

The quote I received for 3' wide and 4' high board with a shortened header and finished as the other boards are is: Boards - $630.00 Crating - $75.00 Brokerage - $135.00 Shipping - $196.50 **Total : $1,036.50** Delivery would be three weeks from order.

¬ Create and distribute a rolling action item list to the team members on a regular basis

¬ Create a "Who's Who" of the team, which contains their photos, name and team. Send team members an email link when new members are added

¬ Create a calendar that shows where everyone is on any given day.

¬ Since teams are located in two separate buildings, which makes face-to-face interaction difficult, it might be helpful to set up a formal schedule of meetings for the team members to meet with one another.

¬ Celebrate milestones – they can be very simple with just a cake, or a tray of cookies or something that brings the team together in one room to celebrate

Bibliography

1. Workplace Bullying Institute & Zogby International, U.S. Workplace Bullying Survey, September 2007, WBI Research Director, Gary Namie, PhD

2. Tim Field, http://www.bullyonline.org

3. Shirer, William (2011-10-23). The Rise and Fall of the Third Reich (pgs. 326, 347, 349). RosettaBooks. Kindle Edition.

4. Workplace bullying: Escalated incivility, By Gary Namie, Reprint # 9B03TF09, Ivey Management Services, November/December 2003, Ivey Business Journal November/December 2003, pg. 3.

5. Sirach. The New American Bible, Revised Edition (NABRE). United States Conference of Catholic Bishops, n.d. Web. 1 Apr. 2014. <http://www.usccb.org/Bible/sirach/26:5>.

6. Westhues, Kenneth. "Mobbing: At the Mercy of the Mob A Summary of Research on Workplace Mobbi." *Www.overcomebullying.org*. Anton Hoyt, n.d. Web. 03 Aug. 2014. <http://www.overcomebullying.org/mobbing-bullying-research.html>.

7. Earl, Jack. Sin – What the Bible Says

8. Kershaw, Alex (2010-10-26). The Envoy: The Epic Rescue of the Last Jews of Europe in the Desperate Closing Months of World War II (p. 125). Perseus Books Group. Kindle Edition.

9. Tim Field, http://www.bullyonline.org/stress/ptsd.htm

10. U.S. Army Survival Manual, Metro Books, New York, an imprint of Sterling Publishing Co., Inc.

41256993R00109

Made in the USA
Middletown, DE
08 March 2017